# *Suicide Risk*
## Assessment

*Practical Strategies and Tools*
*for Joint Commission Compliance*

Lauren R. Ball, MSW, LCSW, BCD

Christina Bivona-Tellez, BSN, MPH, Reviewer

**Suicide Risk Assessment:** *Practical Strategies and Tools for Joint Commission Compliance*
by Lauren R. Ball, MSW, LCSW, BCD

Published by HCPro, Inc. Copyright ©2007 HCPro, Inc.

ISBN 978-1-57839-966-6

HCPro, Inc., provides information resources for the healthcare industry.

HCPro, Inc., is not affiliated in any way with The Joint Commission, which owns the JCAHO trademark.

Lauren R. Ball, MSW, LCSW, BCD, Author
Christina Bivona-Tellez, BSN, MPH, Reviewer
Mary Stevens, Senior Managing Editor
Molly Rowe, Executive Editor
John Novack, Group Publisher
Susan Darbyshire, Cover Designer

Jackie Diehl Singer, Graphic Artist
Jerrie Hildebrand, Layout Artist
Jean St. Pierre, Director of Operations
Darren Kelly, Production Coordinator
Matthew Kuhrt, Copyeditor
Liza Banks, Proofreader

Advice given is general. Readers should consult professional counsel for specific legal, ethical, or clinical questions.

Arrangements can be made for quantity discounts. For more information, contact

HCPro, Inc.
P.O. Box 1168
Marblehead, MA 01945
Telephone: 800/650-6787 or 781/639-1872
Fax: 781/639-2982
E-mail: *customerservice@hcpro.com*

**Visit HCPro at its World Wide Web sites:** *www.hcpro.com* **and** *www.hcmarketplace.com*

02/2007
21090

# Contents

# CONTENTS

# Figures

# About the author

**Lauren R. Ball, MSW, LCSW, BCD**, has worked at Loma Linda University Behavioral Medicine Center in Redlands, CA, since 1994 and currently serves as director of social services and youth services. She has primary responsibility for a 29-bed inpatient unit for children and adolescents, as well as all partial hospital and intensive outpatient mental health and dual-diagnosis programs for approximately 60 outpatient youth and their families.

As director of social services, she also oversees the provision of social services throughout the 89-bed free-standing private psychiatric hospital, which offers specialty units for seniors, adults, and chemical dependency, with associated on-site partial hospital and intensive outpatient mental health and chemical dependency services for adults.

She is a social work field instructor for both Loma Linda University and California State University, San Bernardino, and is an adjunct professor for Duquesne University School of Nursing, in Pittsburgh, PA.

She serves on the Behavioral Health Advisory Committee for the California Hospital Association and is a member of the California Society for Clinical Social Work and the American Psychiatric Nurses Association.

She holds a bachelor's degree in social work from La Sierra University in La Sierra, CA, and a master's degree in social work from Loma Linda University. She is a licensed clinical social worker and a board-certified diplomat in social work.

# About the reviewer

**Christina Bivona-Tellez, BSN, MPH**, is vice president—Inland Office, Hospital Association of Southern California (HASC). Prior to joining the board of HASC, she served for 11 years on both regional and statewide boards for the California Hospital Association (CHA) and HASC, and is past chair of the Behavioral Health Advisory Committee of CHA.

She was a founding staff member of Loma Linda University Behavioral Medicine Center, and has served as adjunct professor at Loma Linda University School of Nursing. She worked closely with sister hospitals of Loma Linda University, serving on nursing leadership and environment–of-care committees.

Previously, she helped open Charter Pines, a free-standing, for-profit hospital in Charlotte, NC, as a nurse manager for adult services, then served as director of nursing services at Charter Lake Hospital in Macon, GA.

She has a bachelor of science—nursing degree from Alfred University, in Alfred, NY, and a masters of public health in nursing administration and maternal and child health from the University of Chapel Hill School of Public Health, in Chapel Hill, NC, with an emphasis in community development and international and cross-cultural health.

# Acknowledgments

Thank you to all those who helped in so many ways with this work.

To Jill Pollock, administrator, Diana Albertson, director of quality resource management, and Ruthita Fike, CEO, for their vision, leadership, mentoring, and dedication to our mission to heal people and restore hope. To the Loma Linda University Behavioral Medicine Center staff for their teamwork, talent, and excellent patient care.

To my husband David, for his daily support and encouragement.

And finally, to all the patients who, for a moment, have allowed me to share in their journey to reignite the spark for life. Your faith, courage, and trust inspire me daily.

# INTRODUCTION

## AN OPPORTUNITY AND A CHALLENGE

# INTRODUCTION

## AN OPPORTUNITY AND A CHALLENGE

Many in the healthcare field were surprised when The Joint Commission included suicide assessment and prevention as a National Patient Safety Goal (NPSG) for 2007. Effective the same year, and equally surprising, was The Joint Commission's announcement that suicide prevention would be one of its first two program-specific tracers.

However, The Joint Commission's decision to address this as a patient safety issue makes sense when you consider these statistics:

- Patient suicide while in a 24-hour staffed-care setting has been the most frequently reported sentinel event since The Joint Commission began tracking such events.[1]

- Overall, suicide is the third-leading cause of death for Americans age 18 and under, and the eleventh most common cause of death for Americans of all ages.[2]

- In 2004, deaths by suicide outnumbered deaths by homicide by a 3 to 2 ratio.[3]

- The rate of suicide for 15- to 24-year-olds has doubled in the United States since the 1960s.[4]

It's still true that many healthcare facilities would rather avoid the subject of patient suicide altogether, but The Joint Commission's acknowledgment of it, via its National Patient Safety Goal, may help many facilities realize that patient suicide is both a compelling patient safety issue and, in many instances, preventable. As hospitals become aware that suicide is a potentially avoidable outcome, they are taking steps to minimize the risk. The NPSG lends new urgency to these efforts.

The Joint Commission's goal requires that hospitals identify safety risks inherent in their patient populations. Identifying patient risk certainly isn't a new idea for most hospitals, and the NPSG complements several standards in The Joint Commission's *Comprehensive Accreditation Manual for Hospitals (CAMH)*. What is new, at least for some facilities, is the explicit application to patient suicide.

Healthcare organizations must also identify individual patients at risk for suicide, and The Joint Commission has indicated that this goal is applicable to

- hospitals with behavioral units
- psychiatric hospitals
- general hospitals that treat patients with emotional or behavioral disorders.

The implementation expectations (IE) for the goal include screening for suicide, an assessment of the patient's immediate safety needs, and providing information to families and patients that can help ensure their safety. It's easy to see why this goal presents a range of troublesome issues for facilities that are developing these tools for the first time.

Further complicating things, The Joint Commission made a suicide assessment and prevention tracer one of its first program-specific tracers.[5]

The obvious questions that have emerged regarding the suicide assessment NPSG are

- Does this goal apply to our hospital?
- How do we identify at-risk patient populations?
- What does an effective risk assessment include?
- What constitutes the safest environment for patients?

As many organizations develop formal screening and risk-assessment policies for the first time, they will likely uncover questions in addition to the ones listed above. Psychiatric hospitals can provide some guidance on suicide screening tools and policy development. However, even with outside help, confronting the issue of patient suicide and finding the information your facility needs might be a challenge for several reasons.

1. **Patient suicide represents the very antithesis of healthcare.** After all, we are the healers, rescuers, and lifesavers. When a patient presents at our doorstep with physical injuries that are beyond repair, or whose illness is too pervasive, or whose condition is just too fragile, we spring into action nonetheless, applying the latest techniques, treatments, surgery, or medications.

   When all the technology, expertise and heroics are not enough, we can usually reconcile ourselves to a "negative outcome." The patient, despite our best efforts, could not be saved, and we understand it to be a tragic but unavoidable loss of life.

   The idea that a patient would want to deliberately, forcefully circumvent all lifesaving efforts seems incomprehensible as well as unconscionable for many in the healthcare profession—even as we work to heal the body, the suicidal patient fights our efforts in his or her attempt (or attempts) to die. If we as healthcare workers can't come to terms with this contradiction and get past our own views on suicide, we run the risk of failing to properly recognize and respond to patients whose greatest risk is themselves.

   When a patient makes the decision to die despite the possibility of recovery—or even lacking any physical ailment at all—what then? While society continues to grapple with these complex cultural and politically charged issues, hospitals must take a preemptive stance to protect lives and provide compassionate, effective care.

2. **Signs of increased suicide risk can be subtle.** A patient's symptoms can be much less obvious than an expressed wish to die. Even at facilities that routinely screen patients for suicide risk, many healthcare workers have not been trained specifically to recognize, assess, and respond effectively to the signs of pain and hopelessness that can potentially be fatal.

   Indeed, some doctors, nurses, and other healthcare staff will actively avoid discussing suicide with their patients, fearful that they might unwittingly plant suicidal ideas in the minds of distraught patients.

3. **There is no such thing as a hazard-free environment.** Providing a safe environment for potentially suicidal patients—while still providing access to the tools, medicines, and equipment necessary for a healthcare setting—presents considerable challenges. The very environment that is designed to facilitate healing can present a cache of potential "resources" for the suicidal patient to end his or her life. Instruments, needles, medicines, and a plethora of medical equipment can become lethal in the hands of someone intent on self-harm. Something as simple as a housekeeper's cart, bed sheet, handrail, power cord, or hospital gown can provide an effective means of suicide to a desperate, suicidal patient. Presumably, this is one reason for The Joint Commission's second IE for this goal.

The risks and challenges are somewhat different for psychiatric facilities than for hospitals with behavioral units. As mentioned earlier, suicide has stubbornly remained the number one sentinel event reported for psychiatric hospitals—even when there is an assumption that a patient may be depressed and suicidal, and the environment has been designed to minimize risks of self-harm, hospitalized patients continue to die from completed suicides.

Even in behavioral settings, there are many instances in which hospital staff are unprepared to differentiate patients who are actually looking for help from those who present the greatest risk for self-harm behaviors or completed suicide.

For example, having one staff member available to monitor a suicidal patient (one-to-one observation) is an effective prevention measure, but one-to-one observation puts a strain on already-stretched staffing resources. Furthermore, it takes time to train staff and make them available for one-to-one patient observation—in some settings, the staff brought in to monitor the potentially suicidal patient might be "floaters" or temporary employees who may not know the patient or treatment plan, or may not have had the same training on suicide risk as core staff.

Finally, with staffing already a challenge in behavioral facilities nationwide and so many other issues demanding immediate attention, it might seem like an impossible challenge to set up a committee, assess an entire facility, and then eliminate as many potential environmental risks for suicidal patients as possible.

Because patients continue to take their own lives even in the facilities that should be best able to prevent this, the NPSG requirement for effective risk assessment is clearly necessary in all behavioral settings.

This Patient Safety Goal also presents opportunities. Addressing and preventing patient suicide is a worthy goal, of course, and now more than ever, psychiatric patient care facilities have an opportunity to help other organizations develop or hone their suicide assessment and prevention programs.

This NPSG also provides all staff—from healthcare leadership to nurses to housekeepers and maintenance workers—with an opportunity to improve patient care. After all, it will take input from every level to effectively screen patients, conduct an environmental assessment, and ensure that workable policies are in place and staff are properly trained to minimize suicidal risks.

Patient suicide can be looked at as one cause of death that is, at least theoretically, totally preventable. The suicidal patient's physical health can be saved if we can recognize, accurately assess, and effectively address the patient's mental health crisis. Conversely, no healthcare setting or intervention can provide an absolute guarantee against a successful suicide. The outcome, ultimately, rests with the patient. Suicidal patients pose a highly lethal, yet potentially curable condition. Healthcare providers must be prepared to recognize patients at risk for suicide, respond to protect them from self-harm, and provide focused and informed interventions to stabilize their psychiatric crisis.

Hospital policies must give staff the training and guidance to maintain an environment and atmosphere that provides the suicidal patient the maximum protective environment and treatment to foster a decision to choose life. Hospitals must also have in place policies that provide direction for wading through the legal, ethical, and moral decision-making involved in treating the suicidal patient seeking to end his or her life.

## Near misses and a call to action

My facility, Loma Linda University Behavioral Medicine Center (LLUBMC), in Redlands, California, took a proactive approach to inpatient suicide well before The Joint Commission announced the 2007 goals. When an LLU administrator asked her directors to list "the three things that keep me awake at night" and bring their list to the administrative council, completed patient suicide was a recurrent theme.

Two nearby hospitals had instances of completed suicides, and two "near misses" at our facility added to the directors' concerns. One patient, intent on escaping the locked unit, knotted his bed sheet, tossed the knot over the bathroom door, then shut it. He barricaded his room, broke out a window, then used the sheet to lower himself down. It was not a suicide attempt, but the same technique could easily have been used for hanging. Another patient had managed, despite the hospital's use of a metal-detecting wand, to smuggle a knife onto the unit. Thankfully, it was discovered soon afterward, but again, the possible outcomes were frightening.

After hearing about the directors' concerns, the potentially tragic near-miss incidents, and the completed suicides at other facilities, plus the fact that patient suicide is the leading sentinel event reported to The Joint Commission, LLU's hospital leadership decided to make suicide prevention their 2005 Failure Modes and Effects Analysis (FMEA) project.

The endeavor touched all areas of the hospital, including

- environment of care
- employee training and assessment
- treatment planning
- patient education
- discharge planning
- contract services such as housekeeping and dietary services

No single committee or task force could complete the task alone: The challenges of such a comprehensive and far-reaching project required the cooperation and coordination of all hospital leadership. It also required the expertise and input of the line staff, who have direct knowledge of the challenges faced and what interventions and changes would really work.

With everyone's help, LLUBMC's FMEA project resulted in improved risk assessments, increased staff training, and a safer environment.

Along with these changes came the awareness at LLUBMC that the job of suicide risk assessment and prevention is an ongoing challenge. Each time a patient attempts self-harm, new information and risks are identified and addressed. Every suicidal event reported to The Joint Commission represents an opportunity to improve safeguards. Hopefully, The Joint Commission's requirements for this NPSG will foster a network of information and ideas from all types of healthcare settings as we face the challenge together.

## How to use this book

In the following pages, you'll find tools, resources, and examples that can help your facility comply with this difficult, yet crucial, National Patient Safety Goal. These chapters will help you

- understand what The Joint Commission's expectations are for this goal

- develop effective risk-assessment and patient-screening tools

- create workable, hospital-specific policies

- conduct an FMEA to gauge your facility's compliance and areas that will need improvement

- assess your facility's physical environment for potential hazards

- foster better communication among staff and with patients

In addition, you'll find information about the suicide-prevention-program tracer, case studies on the FMEA process and environmental assessment, and pages of resources to help you at every step of the way.

The Joint Commission's suicide risk assessment goal presents some unique and daunting challenges. However, like The Joint Commission's other NPSGs, it also offers your facility the opportunity to improve patient care while educating staff and increasing overall awareness of patient suicide—and possibly, preventing a tragedy in the process.

## Endnotes

1. *Reducing the Risk of Suicide,* © 2005. Joint Commission Resources, Inc. (*www.jcr.org*).

2. Ibid.

3. American Association of Suicidology, *Year 2004 Official Final Data on Suicide in the United States,* updated Dec. 15, 2006, *www.suicidology.org/index.cfm.*

4. National Center for Health Statistics, "Suicide Among 15 to 24 Year Olds by Gender, Race/Ethnicity and State 1900 to 2000," *Postsecondary Education Opportunity* 132 (June 2003), *www.postsecondary.org* (accessed December 2006).

5. JCR Inc., "Joint Commission to Implement Program-Specific Tracers in 2007," *Perspectives on JCAHO* 26, no. 11 (November 2006): 4.

# SUICIDE RISK ASSESSMENT GOAL SPECIFICS

# SUICIDE RISK ASSESSMENT GOAL SPECIFICS

Immediately after The Joint Commission announced suicide assessment would be included in the 2007 National Patient Safety Goals (NPSG), healthcare systems across the country began wondering: *Does this goal apply to us? What does The Joint Commission expect us to do?*

Of course, a suicide risk assessment and prevention policy is an integral component of patient care in behavioral facilities, but when is such a policy required for Joint Commission accreditation, and what should it include? This chapter will explore when the suicide-risk assessment NPSG applies.

Joint Commission officials and literature indicate that the first part of the goal—assess risk in your patient populations—is applicable to

- hospitals
- critical-access hospitals
- behavioral healthcare facilities

The applicability of the second part of the goal—which requires organizations to identify patients at risk for suicide—is somewhat less clear. The Joint Commission has indicated that this applies to

- hospitals with behavioral units

- psychiatric hospitals

- general hospitals treating patients with a primary psychiatric condition

According to The Joint Commission, the program-specific tracer for suicide assessment will apply to the same facilities. And commission officials have indicated that the scope of NPSG 15A may be expanded to include other facilities and departments in the future.

Although Joint Commission officials are working to clear up the applicability of this goal, they have also provided differing interpretations of the goal. This has led to confusion, even in facilities which clearly must comply with the goal. The following questions are being asked by staff and leaders in behavioral units across the country:

- Should we screen *all* patients identified as being possibly higher-risk for suicide?

- Should patients diagnosed with a terminal illness be screened?

- What about patients on anti-depressants that have a known possible side effect of inducing suicidal thoughts?

- Do we need to develop one suicide assessment/prevention policy for our entire hospital, or just for the psychiatric unit?

## Scoring expectations

The 2007 scoring methodology changes for the National Patient Safety Goals have raised questions as well. Prior to 2007, all NPSGs were scored at the "A level," requiring 100 percent compliance to avoid a requirement for improvement (RFI). Now, the Joint Commission scores NPSGs the same as it scores other accreditation standards. This could be good news in judging compliance with the suicide risk assessment goal, which has three implementation expectations (IE): 80 percent compliance for the standard may be acceptable ("C" scoring methodology).

However, standard-style scoring also means multiple opportunities for RFI citation.

The IE for this standard include

1. Patients being treated for emotional or behavioral complaints or disorders are assessed for suicide risk. This assessment includes factors that might increase or decrease suicide risk.

2. Steps are taken to reduce any risk of suicide by ensuring the patient is treated in the most appropriate setting and receives appropriate care.

3. The organization provides crisis hotline information to patient and family/caregivers.

Evidence of actions to protect the patient and address safety issues is required. Policies and procedures should be in place to address patient assessment and interventions with at-risk populations. The goal also requires that organizations provide information to patients and families regarding how to respond to crisis situations. And facilities are expected to document their compliance with these policies.

Psychiatric hospitals and behavioral healthcare settings might already have some of these measures in their policies, and it is clear these facilities must comply with this goal—after all, having been diagnosed with a psychiatric illness is the most predictive indicator of a patient's suicide risk.[1] Psychological autopsy reports indicate that more than 90 percent of patients who completed suicide had one or more mental disorders.[2]

Any behavioral health setting that treats patients with mental disorders will need to screen these patients for suicide risk, regardless of whether or not suicide is a part of the presenting problem or the facility's treatment focus. Likewise, some programs that target problems such as eating disorders, dual diagnoses, and geropsychiatric issues may need to evaluate and strengthen their policies and procedures regarding the assessment and reassessment of suicide risks.

## Expectations for hospitals

The suicide risk assessment NPSG's applicability to general hospitals with psychiatric facilities is also relatively straightforward.

If a hospital has an embedded psychiatric unit, this standard applies in all areas of treatment involving psychiatric patients, including

■ When a general hospital has an emergency room that sees patients presenting with psychiatric illness. Most, if not all, emergency departments treat patients who have attempted suicide or are otherwise exhibiting a psychiatric crisis. Some have specialized areas designated for the triage and disposition of psychiatric patients.

■ If the primary reason for a patient's emergency department visit is psychiatric in nature, or if the presenting injury is presumed to be related to a psychiatric illness.

When a patient's clinical presentation indicates mental illness, an assessment of suicide risks and action to protect the safety of the patient is required, regardless of the treatment setting. But what about general hospitals that are treating patients on any of their inpatient units for an injury or condition related to a psychiatric crisis or suicide attempt? For example

- a patient on a burn unit who attempted to immolate himself
- severely injured patients who have cut themselves or intentionally caused an accident
- a patient whose liver is failing following an intentional overdose

In cases where a patient has clearly attempted suicide, an initial screen is not necessary because that patient is already assumed to be at high risk for self-harm. Of course, many cases aren't clearly suicide attempts, and The Joint Commission is expected to provide more details about this goal's applicability as healthcare facilities and surveyors alike become familiar with the issues surrounding this goal. Hospitals should keep an eye on The Joint Commission's Web site (*www.jcaho.org*), along with the *Joint Commission Perspectives* newsletter, and other sources for additional information.

A proactive approach to identifying and responding to suicidal risks is essential for any healthcare organization treating any patient for whom suicide is a part of the clinical presentation. After all, in a general hospital setting, repairing a severed artery is a futile intervention if the suicidal patient's hopelessness and psychic pain are not recognized, and if real help is not offered to ameliorate the suicidal behavior.

## Psychiatric hospital expectations

Behavioral healthcare settings must make a determination at the end of each session or treatment day—"Is my patient stable or safe to go home today?"

Psychiatric hospitals and residential treatment centers must provide an ongoing assessment of risk. Statistics consistently demonstrate that more than half of those completing suicide were being treated for a psychiatric illness at the time of their death.[3]

Joint Commission–accredited behavioral healthcare settings and psychiatric hospitals are expected to provide training to all patient care staff and have some sort of suicide screening and psychiatric consultation available when patients present with suicidal ideation, parasuicidal behaviors, suicide attempt, or current psychiatric illness.

Suicide risk assessment is more than a question of compliance with The Joint Commission's requirements, of course. Considering the statistics regarding suicide rates in general and incidents of suicide while in 24-hour care, it is clear that the problem transcends psychiatric hospitals to include many types of healthcare settings. Ultimately, all healthcare organizations must assess their facility, policies, and staff training protocols regarding suicide risks because it is the right clinical intervention for the patient—in short, it is good clinical practice.

---

### Suicide assessment goal specifics at a glance:

**Goal: The facility identifies risks inherent in its patient population**
- Applies to hospitals, critical access hospitals, behavioral facilities, and home care

**Requirement: The facility identifies patients at risk for suicide**
- Applies to
  - organizations surveyed under the Behavioral Healthcare (BHC) standards, psychiatric hospitals, and general hospitals
  - all patients in psychiatric hospitals
  - general hospital patients whose primary complaint or diagnosis is an emotional or behavioral disorder

**Implementation expectations:**
1. Patients are assessed for suicide risk, including factors that may increase or decrease that risk
2. The facility takes steps to reduce suicide risk by ensuring that the patient is given the most appropriate care in the most appropriate setting
3. The organization provides crisis hotline information to patients and their families/caregivers

---

## Summary

The Joint Commission's suicide risk assessment NPSG requires hospitals with psychiatric units, and those that treat behavioral patients, to develop a patient suicide risk assessment policy. The goal currently does not apply to general hospitals when a patient's primary treatment focus is a medical condition and the hospital lacks any evidence of a current psychiatric condition. However, the goal may eventually be expanded to apply to all settings in all hospitals and other facilities. Additional clarification is likely as surveyors and facilities become familiar with the goal and its implications.

The goal's three IEs include

1. Patients being treated for emotional or behavioral complaints or disorders are to be assessed for suicide risk, including factors that may increase or decrease that risk.

2. Steps are to be taken to reduce any risk of suicide (when assessed) by making sure the patient is in the most appropriate treatment setting and receives appropriate care.

3. The organization provides crisis hotline information to patient and family/caregivers.

The program-specific tracer for suicide assessment will apply to the same facilities to which NPSG 15A applies.

Because additional fine-tuning is likely, it's also a good idea to consult your Joint Commission representative, and keep an eye on the commission's Web site and other resources.

## Endnotes

1. U.S. Department of Health & Human Services, *The Surgeon General's Call to Action to Prevent Suicide 1999, At a Glance: Suicide in the United States* (revised June 2005), *www.surgeongeneral.gov/library/calltoaction/fact1.htm.*

2. American Association of Suicidology, *Year 2003 Official Final Data on Suicide in the United States* (2003), *www.suicidology.org.*

3. Goldsmith, S. K., et al., *Reducing suicide, a national imperative* (Washington, D.C.:The National Academies Press, 2002), *http://books.nap.edu/catalo/10398.html:*13.

# C H A P T E R  T W O

## PATIENT ASSESSMENT BASICS

# PATIENT ASSESSMENT BASICS

## Identifying at-risk hospital patient populations

Many patients will present with suicide attempts that are obvious—a slit wrist, an overdose, an attempted hanging, for example. These attempts may be accompanied by obvious psychiatric symptoms such as delusions, paranoia, or hallucinations.

But how many emergency room patient presentations can be easily overlooked, explained away, or presumed to be an accident? For example, what about

- the patient whose car inexplicably careened off a road?

- the teenager who insists that he was only trying to get high by ingesting a smorgasbord of prescription medications?

- the disheveled elderly gentleman who says that the combination of alcohol and pain medication was a simple mistake?

- the 11-year-old who impulsively darted into the path of an oncoming truck?

What emergency room practitioner, often overwhelmed by the never-ending influx of patients, has the time and training to take a step beyond the explanation, "it was just an accident"? For hospital staff in all areas of care, suicide assessment can put a whole new twist on life-and-death decision-making.

 **TIP** Each person's tolerance for pain, uncertainty, and crisis is unique. Identifying the risk factors in your facility's patient population is a first step in developing a suicide risk assessment, but risk factors alone can't predict which individual patients are in the greatest danger of harming themselves.

Although patient suicide is relatively rare, the mere possibility of it presents great challenges. The line between suicidal thoughts and rational end-of-life decisions can become blurred and conflicting for the healthcare team.

There are also situations where a patient may develop suicidal ideation after being admitted for a non-suicide-related illness. In these cases, suicidal ideation is related to the medical condition being treated. Although the suicide assessment goal's IE for patient screening might not apply to these situations, it's easy to see how these patients could emerge as a population at higher risk for suicide.

## Risk factors to consider

The Joint Commission's NPSG and the American Psychiatric Association Practice Guidelines require facilities to obtain information to identify specific factors and features that may generally increase or decrease risk for suicide or suicidal behaviors.[1] Understanding these factors will help in training all direct-care patient staff to identify patients who fall into higher-risk groups. Identifying multiple risk factors will help you and your staff target in-depth assessments to—and take added precautions with—the patients with the highest risk.

Numerous studies show that suicide is the 11th leading cause of death in the United States, taking roughly 30,000 lives each year, with an estimated 25 suicide attempts for each completed suicide. In addition, as many as 31 percent of the clinical population and 24 percent of the general population have considered suicide at some point in their lives.[2]

Which patients are statistically more likely to consider suicide? Although each of the mental, physical, and demographic populations listed below present unique risks and challenges, the statistics cited here are meant only to assist healthcare professionals in identifying their own patients who are at the highest risk for competing suicide.

**Mental illness** is the first and most predictive factor for suicide risk, as studies repeatedly show. More than 90 percent of individuals who die from suicide have a diagnosable psychiatric disorder, according to the American Psychiatric

Association (APA).[3] Almost all psychiatric disorders, with the exception of mental retardation, are associated with a higher risk of suicide. However, although mental illness is an important indicator, it is also important to note that most people with mental illness never attempt suicide.

The psychiatric disorders most strongly associated with elevated suicide risk are mood disorders. These include bipolar affective disorder, major depressive disorders, and dysthymia (a less-severe and longer-lasting type of depression). The severity and history of the illness over time (i.e., one episode versus recurrent episodes) also affect the overall risk.

The risk of suicide in those with psychotic disorders, especially schizophrenia and schizoaffective disorder, is estimated to be eight times the risk of the general population according to APA data.[4] The risk for schizophrenic patients is highest when there are

- current psychotic symptoms
- past suicide attempts
- a chronic illness
- multiple psychiatric hospitalizations

Within this group, the higher-risk time is in the early years of the disease. Other higher-risk factors for this group include being male, under 30 years of age, and being socially isolated.[5]

In addition to mood disorders and psychotic disorders, anorexia and certain other personality disorders (e.g., borderline personality disorder, narcissism, etc.) are also associated with higher risk of suicide in many studies.

**Substance abuse** is another important risk factor. Alcohol-use disorders are present in about 25 percent of all completed suicides in the United States. Alcohol intoxication is a factor in 64 percent of suicides.[6] Other substance-abuse disorders indicate higher suicide risk as well.

**Hopelessness** is associated with suicide and suicidal behaviors across all populations, risk factors, and age groups.

Other psychological factors associated with elevated suicide risk include anxiety and panic attacks, shame, psychological turmoil or psychic pain, impulsiveness, aggression, poor self-esteem, and agitation.

Each of these factors is significant and indicates a higher potential for suicide risk when present. When more than one of these factors is present, this indicates a patient at higher risk.

## Demographic factors

Mental illness can be an important indicator of potential suicide risk, but it is not the only factor by any means. Furthermore, there is usually interplay among these factors, as well as among demographic, psychological, and physical factors. The skilled assessor will need to look at the complete picture when determining the potential risk of these factors, and how they affect a facility's patient population.

**Age.** It has long been known certain age groups are statistically at higher suicide risk than others. From age 10–24, the overall death rate from suicide tends to be around 13 per 100,000 population, and stays relatively level through middle age. However, around age 70, the suicide rate again begins to climb: statistically, the highest-risk age group for suicide deaths is 75 and older. This group represents 13 percent of the general population, yet it accounts for nearly 20 percent of suicide deaths.

For men age 85 and older, the suicide rate jumps to nearly 48 per 100,000. 70 percent of elderly suicide victims have visited a physician within a month of committing suicide.[7]

| Figure 2.1 | **DEMOGRAPHIC RISK FACTORS** |
|---|---|

- Age
- Gender
- Race, culture, and ethnicity
- Marital status, sexual orientation, and occupation
- Trauma and violence
- Physical illness
- Family history of suicide

Among the general population age 15–24, suicide is now the third-leading cause of death, with a total of 3,971 suicides in this group in 2001.[8] Although suicide rates overall have remained relatively stable, the rate for this age group has tripled since the 1950s. Suicide among adolescents is often an impulsive act following a stressful event, such as getting into trouble at school or with law enforcement, a relationship breakup, or an argument with friends or family.

**Gender.** Death by suicide is more common among men than women in the United States. The death rate for men is approximately four times greater than that of women. However, women are three times more likely than men to attempt suicide. The disparity of these statistics is related to the fact that women tend to use less-lethal methods when making suicide attempts. They also have fewer incidences of substance abuse and tend to be less impulsive than their male counterparts.[9]

**Race, culture, and ethnicity.** The incidence of suicide is consistently highest among Caucasians in the United States, and second-highest among Native American and Alaskan Native populations. Pacific Islanders and Asian, black, and Hispanic populations have lower suicide rates, although significant differences among men and women in these groups exist regarding suicide risk. For example, Hispanic men have a higher suicide rate than Hispanic women, while Asian women have a higher rate than Asian men.[10]

Different cultures and religions have widely varying views of suicide. In some cultures, suicide may be seen as an acceptable response to shame, some types of personal crises, and physical illness. Help-seeking behavior also differs among cultures, with some groups avoiding disclosure of suicidal thoughts or behaviors.

**Marital status, sexual orientation, and occupation.** Many studies indicate that single people commit suicide significantly more often than those who are married. The rate among those who are divorced, separated, or widowed is also significantly higher than among those who are married.

The affect of sexual orientation on suicide risk is less clear. Some studies note an increased risk of suicidal behavior among gays and lesbians, especially in younger populations. Some studies indicate that stressors such as disclosure of sexual orientation to family and harassment due to sexual orientation contribute to gay and lesbian suicide as well, but these factors require further study.

Some occupations have statistically higher rates of suicide, although this is affected by socio-economic, gender, age, and ethnic differences in certain occupations. According to APA findings, risk is highest among

- dentists and physicians
- nurses
- social workers
- artists

- mathematicians
- scientists[11]

Unemployment increases the risk of both suicide attempts and completed suicides, particularly in the time period closest to the loss of employment, and in people age 45 and younger. For those who are unemployed, other stresses, such as financial difficulties and marital stress, may also increase the risk, according to the APA.

**Trauma and violence.** Having a childhood history of trauma, physical abuse and/or sexual abuse has been shown in several studies to increase the risk of suicide as much as tenfold. Abuse in childhood also increases the risk for self-injurious behaviors, and suicidal gestures and ideations.[12] The severity and duration of the abuse correlates to higher risk.

A history of experiencing domestic violence is associated with higher incidences of suicide attempts and ideation. Risks are also increased for perpetrators and for children who have been witnesses to domestic violence.

**Physical illness.** Several illnesses have been associated with increased risk for suicide. Beyond that, however, physical illnesses may lead to other risk factors, such as depression, financial stress, and job loss. A loss of independence, significant functional impairment, pain, and disfigurement resulting from illness or injury also increase a patient's risk of suicide.

**Family history of suicide.** Multiple studies have shown that the risk of suicide and suicidal behaviors is greater in people who have relatives who have committed suicide. The hereditary and environmental factors that place one person at high suicide risk can also affect other family members subjected to these same influences.

## Protective factors

The Joint Commission's implementation expectations for the suicide risk assessment NPSG stipulate that facilities identify factors that may decrease suicide risk as well. The Centers for Disease Control (CDC) has identified several protective factors, including

- care for mental, physical, and substance-abuse disorders
- access to clinical interventions and support
- support from family and community
- ongoing, supportive medical and mental healthcare relationships
- ability to solve problems, resolve conflicts, handle disputes in a nonviolent way
- cultural and religious beliefs that discourage suicide[13]

Protective factors can serve to decrease a patient's suicide risk, especially when several of these factors are present.

## Summary

Although each patient much be considered individually, a variety of physical, mental, and demographic factors have been identified as factors that can elevate a patient's risk of suicide. It's important to understand which of these factors is most likely to be present in your patient population. These risk factors can't reliably predict which particular patient will be at greatest risk for attempting suicide, but if a patient presents with several of these factors, his or her suicide risk is statistically higher than for patients who aren't part of these groups.

Facilities should also identify the protective factors present among their patients that lower the risk of suicide.

## Endnotes

1. See The Joint Commission's Web site at *www.jointcommission.org* for exact wording of NPSGs. See also American Psychiatric Association, *Practice Guideline for the Assessment and Treatment of Patients With Suicidal Behaviors* (November, 2003), *www.psych.org*.

2. Linehan, M.M., Laffaw, J.A., *Suicidal behaviors among clients at an outpatient psychology clinic versus the general population*, Suicide and Life-threatening Behavior, 12(4), 234-9, Winter 1982.

3–5. American Psychiatric Association, *Practice Guideline for the Assessment and Treatment of Patients with Suicidal Behaviors* (November 2003), *www.psych.org*.

6. Suicide Prevention Resource Center, "Substance Use Disorders and Suicide," from U.S. Department of Health and Human Services, Public Health Service, *National Strategy for Suicide Prevention: Goals and Objectives for action* (2001), *www.sprc.org.*

7. Steven E. Hyman, M.D., *Testimony on Suicide Awareness and Prevention*, testimony before the Senate Committee on Appropriations, Subcommittee on Labor, Health and Human Services, Education (February 8, 2000) *www.hhs.gov/asl/testify/t000208b.html.* Accessed December 2006.

8–10, 13. Centers for Disease Control's National Center for Injury Prevention and Control, Suicide: Fact Sheet, *www.cdc.gov/ncipc/factsheets/suifacts.htm.*

11. APA, *Practice Guideline for the Assessment and Treatment of Patients with Suicidal Behaviors* (November 2003), *www.apa.psych.org.*

12. Ibid.

# ASSESSING RISKS

# ASSESSING RISKS

One of the biggest challenges in screening for suicide risk is determining what patients present the greatest risk of suicide *completion*. For example, should an adolescent girl with superficial wounds on her wrists receive same care precautions as an 80-year-old widowed man who has only said he wishes to kill himself?

After all, both of these patients belong to higher-risk populations, according to a multitude of studies. This example illustrates the kind of tough questions many healthcare workers face—questions that can only be answered through accurate patient assessment.

Patient assessment is closely related to the identification of risk in patient populations. According to Joint Commission literature, one rationale for the suicide assessment NPSG is that identifying individuals at risk for suicide while in the care of a healthcare organization is an important first step in protecting at-risk individuals and planning their care.[1]

When you've identified the higher-risk populations among your patients and made staff aware of risk factors, the next step is to use that information to develop ways to assess individual patients for suicide risk more accurately.

Patient suicide risk assessment is an ongoing process that includes

- initial screen
- comprehensive assessment (if indicated)
- reassessment

As you build or fine-tune the components of the assessment process, keep these important cautions in mind, and make sure the staff members who care for patients are also aware of these caveats:

**One size doesn't fit all.** Initial suicide risk screens may be useful in determining overall suicidal ideation and risk, but they have not been shown to predict with certainty an individual patient's suicide risk. Screening tools are no substitute for clinical assessment.

**Asking questions may not be enough.** Some patients will deny suicidal intentions, so asking them whether they want to harm themselves won't provide an accurate assessment. Likewise, a patient's denial of intent should not be construed as an assurance that the patient will be safe.

A skilled interviewer can establish rapport and elicit accurate information from patients, but when skilled staff are not available to conduct a patient assessment, you can't depend solely on questioning the patient. Whenever possible, staff members conducting an initial screening should consider additional information such as

- the nature of the patient's injuries
- current family/home/work situation
- psychiatric history
- substance abuse

## Circumstances are part of patient assessment

If a patient is admitted following a suicide attempt, the potential lethality of that attempt should also be considered, because it can demonstrate how serious the patient is about taking his or her life. A large number of studies show, for example, that the two most lethal methods of suicide are the use of firearms and hanging—both of these types of attempts must be seen as a clear intention to die, and strong precautions are indicated. Data also show that overdoses and cutting tend to be less-lethal methods, although individual circumstances vary.

The setting should also be considered: How likely was it that the patient would be discovered in his or her suicide attempt? Attempts that are made when no one is likely to be present to prevent or respond to the attempt should also be considered as clear intent to die. Stronger suicide precautions are indicated than if a patient attempted suicide in such a way that he or she would likely be discovered.

## Screening, assessing, and reassessing

When possible, initial patient screening should be done at admission. Different facilities have varying policies regarding initial assessments at other times during care, and their guidelines for comprehensive assessment and reassessment also vary. In psychiatric facilities, screening and subsequent assessment should be considered

- at admission
- when a patient's functioning changes
- when a change in the level of treatment is considered
- prior to discharge

The American Psychiatric Association's practice guidelines recommend that facilities conduct a suicide risk assessment in additional situations as well:

- during ED or crisis evaluation

- in anticipation or experience of a significant loss or psychosocial stressor (e.g., divorce, financial loss, legal problems, etc.)

- with a diagnosis of a serious physical illness (particularly those that are life-threatening, disfiguring, or associated with severe pain or loss of functions)[2]

In all facilities, overt suicidal statements and suicidal behaviors must be taken seriously and will require additional assessment and reassessment throughout the patient's stay. The presence of suicidal ideation and intent should be included in the initial assessment for all behavioral health settings at admission and again prior to discharge for all 24-hour settings. General hospitals might choose to screen patients for suicide risk if they present with mental health issues and additional demographic factors discussed in Chapter 2.

For behavioral health settings, patients often are admitted following a suicide attempt or intense suicidal ideation. However, it is important to note that fewer than half of inpatient suicides were admitted with known suicidal ideation, and only one-fourth were admitted after a suicide attempt.[3] Therefore, it is imperative that *all* patients admitted to psychiatric units be assessed on an ongoing basis for suicidal risk.

An important distinction to make here is the risk presented by suicide completers, versus suicide attempters. For every completed suicide, there are an estimated 25 attempted suicides.[4] There is also growing concern over patients who engage in self-injurious behaviors that apparently are not accompanied by suicidal thoughts or intent.

Based on the information above, it follows that patients should be further assessed when

- **there is a reasonable assumption that the patient has made an attempt to harm himself or herself** (including all cases of overdose, alcohol poisoning, and ingestion of toxic materials)

- **the patient reports suicidal thoughts or intent**, or the patient's family is concerned about the person being suicidal

- **the patient has a psychiatric illness and/or a substance abuse issue**

- **the patient is in a high-risk group for suicidal behavior**

This evaluation helps identify when to use additional precautions and can help facilities assess for the appropriate level of care, complying with the goal's second implementation expectation. The results of the screen could trigger a more in-depth assessment by the treatment team while allowing for immediate implementation of risk-reduction strategies. (Chapter 4 includes additional recommendations for initial screens, and comprehensive assessment and reassessment tools.)

## Summary

Understanding your facility's higher-risk patient populations can help you and your staff determine which patients to assess for suicide risk—the "who" and the "when"—but is not a fail-safe method of determining which patients present the greatest risk of self-harm.

Patient assessment should be approached as an ongoing process, from an initial risk screen to more comprehensive assessment, to reassessment, throughout the care continuum, and should be documented both to show compliance with the goal and to foster strong communication among all staff caring for the patient (see Chapter 6 for more about the role of good communication in suicide risk assessment and prevention).

An initial suicide-risk screen should be a matter of course for patients at psychiatric facilities, because mental illness is a major contributor to heightened suicide risk. General hospital EDs should screen patients who present with psychiatric issues, and obtain an in-depth assessment as soon as possible for those being treated for definite suicide-attempt-related injuries.

If you're confident that your facility understands who should be assessed and when, it's time to look at how to conduct your assessment. Chapter 4 explores what your risk-assessment tools should include.

## Endnotes

1. The Joint Commission, *CAMH Update* 2. (JCR Inc. 2006).

2. American Psychiatric Association, *Practice Guideline for the Assessment and Treatment of Patients with Suicidal Behaviors* (November 2003), *www.psych.org*.

3. Ibid.

4. American Association of Suicidology, *Year 2003 Official Final Data on Suicide in the United States* (2003), *www.suicidology.org*.

C H A P T E R    F O U R

## SCREENING TOOL ESSENTIALS

# SCREENING TOOL ESSENTIALS

Earlier chapters covered risk factors that can help you understand which patients in your system might present the greatest potential suicide risk. Now that you've identified pertinent risk factors for your population, it's time to develop or fine-tune your initial patient suicide-risk assessment tool. You must also understand what your screening tool can (and can't) do.

The Joint Commission doesn't specify what that initial screen must include—rather, surveyors want to know that a screen is implemented that will assess patients' suicide risk as effectively as possible. They will look for evidence that staff are familiar with the screen, know when a patient should be screened, and do so.

 **TIP**  Keep your initial risk assessment as short as possible, and make it easy for all staff to use

The length of this initial assessment varies from setting to setting, and can range from four or five questions to 10.

The initial screen for patients should be as short as possible, usable by medical and non-medical staff alike, and should include, at a minimum, these basic questions or variations on them:

- **Is there a reasonable assumption that the patient has made an attempt to harm himself or herself?** Include all cases of overdose, alcohol poisoning, and ingestion of toxic materials.

- **Does the patient report suicidal thoughts or intent?** Is the patient's family aware/concerned that he or she is suicidal?

- **Does the patient report feeling hopeless?**

- **Does the patient have a psychiatric illness and/or a substance abuse issue?**

- **Is this patient in a group at higher risk for suicidal behaviors than others?**

Different settings modify these questions to suit their staff mix and patient populations. An inpatient psychiatric unit, which includes many mental health professionals, might have a longer list of questions and may designate staff for screening. Out of necessity, a screening tool for an ED might be shorter, and include questions that any emergency staff member could ask. For example, one study concluded that an urban emergency department's screening tool for children and adolescents presenting for primarily psychiatric reasons should address these four issues:

- current suicidal behavior
- past suicidal behavior
- past self-destructive behavior
- current stressors[1]

Some screens, such as the well-known SAD PERSONS scale[2] and variations, weight the answers to basic questions with numeric values; patients who score above a certain number are considered to be at an elevated risk for suicide, and additional precautions are activated. In other facilities, the basic screen might include yes/no checkboxes; and a designated number of yes answers might trigger additional preventive measures.

A wide variety of resources is available to help you build your screen or to adapt a tool developed elsewhere. See Appendix A at the end of this book, consult your state hospital association, and if possible, investigate the screening tools that other hospitals have developed in your area.

 **TIP** The initial screen can be a removable part of a larger, more in-depth risk assessment.

At Loma Linda University Behavioral Medicine Center, we chose to develop our own quick screening tool as part of a larger risk assessment (see **Figure 4.1** for a sample of an initial suicide screening tool developed at LLUBMC). The initial screen helps to identify when to use additional precautions and assists caregivers in determining the appropriate level of care for the patient. The results of the screen can trigger a more in-depth assessment by the treatment team while allowing for immediate implementation of risk-reduction strategies.

The screen used by LLUBMC is a part of the initial patient assessment, and is also available for reassessing the patient at different points during treatment and prior to discharge, enabling staff to adjust suicide precautions up or down if necessary. The treating physician or therapist determines what course of action to take after the initial assessment.

Our facility needed a screen that was as accurate as possible while being simple enough for assessment clinicians to add to the other assessment information being taken at admission. Although much of the same information is available in various other places on the initial patient assessment, we decided it would be helpful to have all the risk factors listed on the suicide risk screen, because this screen clarifies the clinical picture specific to suicide risk.

## Constructing the screen

Development of the screen was a multidisciplinary and interdepartmental process: The director of the inpatient suicide FMEA project developed the screening tool, which was submitted to the patient-care committee. (See Chapter 7 for more about the FMEA process.) The screen was piloted to the intake department, charge nurses, and outpatient therapists for feedback, then submitted to attending physicians.

 **TIP**   To build an effective screening tool
1. Gather data about risk factors/patient population
2. Assign values to risk factors
3. Seek input about your screen's usability
4. Revise as necessary

First, we gathered data on risk factors, predictors, and protective factors related to suicide. We looked at the American Psychiatry Association's Practice Guidelines, The Joint Commission's Sentinel Event Alert on inpatient suicide, and the American Association of Suicidology and Suicide Prevention Resource Center Web sites.

Next, we rank-ordered the risk factors that applied to patients in our facility, mocked up a risk screen, and had our attending psychiatrists and LLUBMC research committee review it. This screening tool can be adapted for other facilities.

| Figure 4.1 |
| :--: |

# SAMPLE SUICIDE RISK SCREEN

| RISK FACTOR | LOWER RISK | MILD RISK | MODERATE RISK | HIGH RISK |
| --- | --- | --- | --- | --- |
| Intent/Ambience | ❏ No intent to die | ❏ Minimal intent | ❏ **Moderate\* intent** | ❏ **Clear intent\*\*** |
| Lethality of attempt (or Plan) | ❏ None/Ideation only | ❏ Gesture | ❏ **Non-lethal\*** | ❏ **Potentially lethal (esp., firearm, hanging, OD)\*\*** |
| Prior attempts | ❏ 2–10 years ago | ❏ 1–2 years ago | ❏ **6–12 mos ago\*** | ❏ **1 wk – 6 mos ago\*\*** |
| Hopelessness | ❏ Hopeful | ❏ Some hope | ❏ **Ambivalent\*** | ❏ **Hopeless\*\*** |
| Substance abuse | ❏ None | ❏ Recreational | ❏ **Abuse\*** | ❏ **Dependence\*** |
| Support system | ❏ Good support | ❏ Some support | ❏ **Conflicted\*** | ❏ **None\*** |
| Current stressor severity | ❏ None | ❏ Mild | ❏ **Moderate\*** | ❏ **Severe\*** |
| Loss & trauma (past 6 mos) | ❏ None | ❏ Moderate | ❏ **Serious\*** | ❏ **Multiple\*** |
| Gender | ❏ Female | | ❏ Male | |
| Age | ❏ 1–15 | ❏ 15–24 | ❏ 24–69 | ❏ 70+ |
| Marital status | ❏ Married/Partner | ❏ Single | ❏ Divorced | ❏ Widowed |
| Sexual orientation | ❏ Heterosexual | | ❏ Gay/Lesbian or Bisexual | |
| Ethnicity | ❏ Non-white/ black | | ❏ White | |
| Chronic/severe illness and/or functional impairment | ❏ None | ❏ Acute illness and/or mild functional impairment | ❏ Chronic illness and/or mild functional impairment | ❏ Chronic illness and/or moderate-to-severe functional impairment |

Patients with multiple risk factors, especially when presenting with psychiatric illness, substance abuse and co-morbid conditions, should be assessed further for suicide risk and necessary precautions. *Consider the total number and severity of all risk factors.*

   \* Risk Factors in | striped bordered area | may indicate need for further assessment.

\*\*   Risk Factors in | solid bordered area | indicate cause for <u>immediate assessment</u> of risk and intervention.

*NOTE: This tool is designed to screen for demographic factors that may help identify patients who fall into a statistically higher risk group for self-harm. This tool is not intended to be a definitive or comprehensive assessment. Patients with higher scores should be assessed further for necessary level of care to minimize the risk of self-harm.*

Staff member signature: _____      Date/Time: _____

*Source: LLUBMC. Reprinted with permission.*

# Who should screen patients

Depending on your patient population, the use of a suicide assessment screen should be considered at these points in treatment:

- At admission
- when a patient's functioning changes
- when a change in the level of treatment is considered
- prior to discharge
- And at other times as determined by the treating clinicians

All patients admitted to LLUBMC are presumed to be in a high-risk category due to their admitting diagnosis and current psychiatric crisis, and are therefore screened for suicide risk as part of the admission process. Substance-abuse patients are also considered high risk and are screened at admission, as are patients attending outpatient programs (e.g., Partial Hospital Program and Intensive Outpatient Program for children, adolescents, adults, and those with chemical dependency).

The psychiatrist or therapist at LLUBMC conducts an initial interview and mental-status exam that addresses current and past suicidal ideation, attempts, and intent, along with psychiatric history. However, this evaluation may not occur immediately on admission. In the case of an after-hours admission, intake staff may admit the patient to an outpatient program, but make an appointment for the next treatment day, at which time the therapist would assess the patient.

The initial screen helps identify patients who fall into a group that has a statistically higher risk for self-harm. It can also help staff decide whether to use additional precautions, and can assist caregivers in determining the appropriate level of care for the patient. The results of the screening would trigger a more in-depth assessment by the treatment team while allowing for immediate implementation of risk-reduction strategies.

## What a screening tool cannot do

■ **Replace a more complete assessment by a physician or mental health professional.**

As one study states: "There are a variety of suicide assessment and risk-screen tools to use. Each of them has advantages depending on the setting in which they are used, the populations to be screened, and the skill level of those using the tool. [However], it should be emphasized that the evaluation of a patient's risk for suicide should never be based upon a score on a single scale. Rather, a comprehensive assessment should be conducted in order to evaluate an individual's risk for suicide. Such an evaluation should include an assessment of many risk factors for suicide."[2]

■ **Identify every potentially suicidal patient.** A one-size-fits-all screen for patient risk won't work, because each patient's circumstances are unique. For reasons explained in earlier chapters, a preliminary screen cannot gauge suicidal ideation with 100 percent accuracy. It should be treated as a way of alerting staff to patients who may be at higher risk for suicide than the general patient population.

■ **Serve as a complete suicide assessment policy.** A good screening tool can help your facility comply with The Joint Commission's NPSG for suicide risk, but must be integrated into a more comprehensive policy to be truly effective at suicide prevention. See Appendix B for a list of standards required for hospitals under the commission's *Comprehensive Accreditation Manual for Hospitals.*

## Summary

The Joint Commission doesn't tell you exactly what to put into your initial screening tool, but does expect it to cover your patient population. Your initial suicide-screening tool should be short, concise, and easy to use for all staff who might need it, regardless of whether they work in the ED, ICU, behavioral units, or admissions.

At a minimum, every initial screening tool should address these questions:

- Do you feel hopeless?
- Do you have a desire to harm or kill yourself?
- Have you experienced a recent traumatic loss?
- Mental illness/substance abuse issues

The questions can be tailored to individual facilities or healthcare systems, and the tool can be included with admission forms or other assessments. Whether you assign a numeric value to each question or gauge the patient's risk by the number of yes versus no answers, your screen should specify what actions to take if a substantial suicide risk is indicated.

A more in-depth assessment should follow the initial screen if the first screen indicates that a patient might have an elevated suicide risk. Patients who are shown to be at risk should be reassessed at various points during their treatment.

It's important to remember that a screening tool won't catch every patient who's potentially suicidal, won't replace a thorough patient assessment, and is only one component of a comprehensive suicide assessment and prevention policy.

# Endnotes

1. Horowitz, L.M.; Wang, P.S.; Koocher, G.P., et al, "Detecting suicide risk in a pediatric emergency department: development of a brief screening tool," *Pediatrics* 107 no. 5 (2001):1133-7, *www.pediatrics.org*.

2. Patterson, W.M.; Dohn, H.H.; Bird, J.; Patterson, G.A., "Evaluation of Suicidal Patients: The SAD PERSONS Scale," *Psychosomatics* 24 no. 4 (1983):343-349. Cited by many other online and print resources.

3. Gregory K. Brown, Ph.D., *A Review of Suicide Assessment Measures for Intervention Research with Adults and Older Adults,* (University of Pennsylvania, Philadelphia:1999). Accessed from the National Institutes of Mental Health Web site, *www.nimh.gov*, December 2006.

# C H A P T E R    F I V E

## COMMUNICATION

# COMMUNICATION

Effective communication is imperative to good care in any healthcare setting, especially when patients at risk for suicide are part of the population. When patients may not be cooperative with treatment and may purposely attempt to find ways to circumvent treatment and hurt themselves, communication among everyone involved with the patient becomes even more important.

## Communication among staff

When your hospital's suicide risk screen identifies an at-risk patient, staff must know what steps to take next to ensure that the patient receives care in the most appropriate setting -- the goal's second IE. Compliance with this IE will depend on effective communication. Caregivers and other staff must have some way of quickly identifying at-risk patients; patient information must be communicated as shifts change; and the patient's condition, treatment, and precautions must be thoroughly documented.

Communication of patient information among caregivers as it relates to suicide risk is critical when treating patients at risk for suicide. Statistics bear out how important good communication is: From 1995–2004, a lack of or incomplete communication was the fourth-leading factor in root cause analyses (RCAs) of inpatient suicide. In 2005, it moved up to number three.[1]

The suicidal patient requires constant monitoring and evaluation of his or her environment for potential hazards. Patient flow sheets and nursing change-of-shift reports, as well as MD-to-MD hand-offs and other staff shift changes, are times when the patient's status must be communicated completely and accurately to the next caregiver.

**TIP** Documented information keeps lines of communication open among staff on different shifts. Make sure your documentation of assessment, reassessment, precautionary steps taken, environmental threats addressed, and contact with family is as complete as possible.

**Everyone who has contact with the patient must be aware of the risks and precautions that need to be taken for patient safety.** A maintenance worker who leaves tools unattended in a patient area, a dietary worker placing a knife on a dinner tray, a housekeeper who doesn't noticing missing sheets, or a family member bringing in a glass vase of flowers can all unwittingly provide the suicidal patient with access to dangerous items. Likewise, a caregiver leaving a patient alone "just for a minute," or allowing the door to the bathroom to be shut can also create a dangerous opportunity for self-harm.

These communication needs can present a considerable challenge when also providing for patient confidentiality and privacy. Some emergency departments have developed "safe rooms" that are designed specifically for the safety of patients at risk of self-harm. All staff are made aware that patients in these rooms are at high risk and require special safety precautions.

In general hospitals, noting suicidal patients' condition on medical, surgical, and ICU units may be more challenging.

Some ways to note that a patient has been identified as a suicide risk include

- colored armbands or hospital gowns
- colored stickers on patient charts
- alert "flags" on patient doors

These signals can alert all staff who will be interacting with the at-risk patient. But whatever method you use, make sure all staff understand the designation.

**Communication is integral to effective monitoring.** In psychiatric facilities as well as general hospitals, certain rooms in close proximity to the nurses' station can be designated for patients considered to be at highest suicide risk. Often these patients require increased or one-to-one staffing. Each new caregiver should be given a report on the specific risks of the particular patient and his or her current status.

Reassessment of suicidal thoughts and behaviors should be conducted and com-municated each shift, or whenever there is a change in caregivers (for example, during breaks) at a minimum. LLUBMC uses a 1:1 observation sheet that docu-ments the patient's location, affect, behaviors, activities, visitors, interventions, and response at 15-minute intervals. (See **Figure 5.1**.)

Outpatients at LLUBMC who are deemed to be at increased risk of suicidal behavior have a colored sticker placed on their chart to help alert all members of the treatment staff to the increased risk. Clinicians assess suicide risk on a daily basis, either by face-to-face interview or using a self-report tool,[2] and chart the patient's status regularly. In addition, patients at risk, as a condition of admission, must acknowledge and allow family members to be involved and informed regarding any changes, risks, and recommendations.

LLUBMC outpatient programs have the advantage of being attached to the university-based teaching psychiatric hospital, so psychiatric consultations and assessments for possible hospitalization are available within minutes. Facilities that don't have psychiatric units will need to develop systems of communication with outside entities to provide support services.

## Communication with the patient

The third IE for the suicide assessment goal is that hospitals will provide suicide/crisis hotline information to patients and their families at discharge—a requirement for direct communication between the facility and the patient.

**Figure 5.1**

# SAMPLE PATIENT OBSERVATION SHEET

**CODES**

**DATE:** _____

**Location Codes**

B = Bed
RBR = Bathroom
CR = Consultation Room
D = Day Room
E = Exam Room
G = Gym
GR = Group Room
H = Hallway
O = Off-campus appointment
OR = Observation Room
OT = Occupational Therapy Room
PT = Patio
QR = Quiet Room
R = Patient Room
S = School
WD = Washer/dryer Room

**Location Codes**

1 = Awake
2 = Asleep
3 = Quiet
4 = Agitated
5 = With MD
6 = With Staff
7 = Interaction with peers
8 = TV, music, reading
9 = personal hygiene
10 = Visitors
11 = Group
12 = Eating
13 = Telephone
14 = Withdrawal
15 = Smoking
16 = Other
17 = Other

**Observation level**

1:1 – Ordered by Physician; document O2h on Progress Notes

X – Seclusion/restraint; document Observation Level only, use Seclusion and Restraint Record for detail

| | Obs. level code | Location | Activity | Initials | | Obs. level code | Location | Activity | Initials |
|---|---|---|---|---|---|---|---|---|---|
| 0000 AM | | | | | 0000 PM | | | | |
| 0015 | | | | | 0015 | | | | |
| 0030 | | | | | 0030 | | | | |
| 0045 | | | | | 0045 | | | | |
| 0100 | | | | | 0100 | | | | |
| 0115 | | | | | 0115 | | | | |
| 0130 | | | | | 0130 | | | | |
| 0145 | | | | | 0145 | | | | |
| 0200 | | | | | 0200 | | | | |
| 0215 | | | | | 0215 | | | | |
| 0230 | | | | | 0230 | | | | |
| 0245 | | | | | 0245 | | | | |
| 0300 | | | | | 0300 | | | | |
| 0315 | | | | | 0315 | | | | |
| 0330 | | | | | 0330 | | | | |
| 0345 | | | | | 0345 | | | | |
| 0400 | | | | | 0400 | | | | |
| 0415 | | | | | 0415 | | | | |
| 0430 | | | | | 0430 | | | | |
| 0445 | | | | | 0445 | | | | |
| 0500 | | | | | 0500 | | | | |
| 0515 | | | | | 0515 | | | | |
| 0530 | | | | | 0530 | | | | |
| 0545 | | | | | 0545 | | | | |
| 0600 | | | | | 0600 | | | | |
| 0615 | | | | | 0615 | | | | |
| 0630 | | | | | 0630 | | | | |
| 0645 | | | | | 0645 | | | | |
| 0700 | | | | | 0700 | | | | |
| 0715 | | | | | 0715 | | | | |
| 0730 | | | | | 0730 | | | | |
| 0745 | | | | | 0745 | | | | |
| 0800 | | | | | 0800 | | | | |
| 0815 | | | | | 0815 | | | | |
| 0830 | | | | | 0830 | | | | |
| 0845 | | | | | 0845 | | | | |
| 0900 | | | | | 0900 | | | | |
| 0915 | | | | | 0915 | | | | |
| 0930 | | | | | 0930 | | | | |
| 0945 | | | | | 0945 | | | | |
| 1000 | | | | | 1000 | | | | |
| 1015 | | | | | 1015 | | | | |
| 1030 | | | | | 1030 | | | | |
| 1045 | | | | | 1045 | | | | |
| 1100 | | | | | 1100 | | | | |
| 1115 | | | | | 1115 | | | | |
| 1130 | | | | | 1130 | | | | |
| 1145 | | | | | 1145 | | | | |

Patient Identification_____

Source: LLUBMC. Adapted with permission.

It's also important to communicate clearly and keep the patient informed of what's happening at all times. Include the patient in planning for his or her safety and determining the appropriate level of care. Necessary interventions can feel punitive to the patient if he or she does not understand why things are being done. For example, if the assessment indicates that the patient should not have access to certain items, explain what is being done and why when belts, shoelaces, sharps, etc. are being removed from the room. If the patient needs one-to-one supervision, be frank about why the supervision is necessary and what he or she can and cannot do privately.

For outpatient programs, patients must have a plan and a method to contact treatment professionals after hours. Upon admission, emergency contingencies should be discussed and outlined in the treatment plan. Patients should be given a list of emergency contact numbers, as well as a plan to contact family members as needed.

An initial "safety plan" can outline emergency plans and communication channels for use if the patient experiences a suicidal crisis. This does not mean that an outpatient therapist must be available by phone 24/7, although some choose to do this. It does mean that the patient must have a way of accessing help at all times, whether it be by contact with the clinician, family member, crisis hotline, 911, or local emergency room. At least one designated family member or significant person should be involved in and aware of emergency contingencies.

At LLUBMC, we have developed several effective ways to do this:

■ Emergency contact information is preprinted on all discharge plans, including psychiatric inpatient, chemical dependency, and all outpatient programs.

■ In addition, a wallet-sized emergency card is provided to the patient (see **Figure 5.2**).

■ All outpatient therapists at LLUBMC have a phone message that gives emergency crisis information and an option to be immediately connected with the hospital's 24-hour assessment line. In addition, outpatients are asked to provide treatment staff with the phone number of a family member/significant other to be contacted by the treatment staff if an emergency exists.

■ If a patient deemed to be at high risk for suicide fails to show up for treatment and cannot be reached at any of the contact numbers, a family member is contacted to check on the patient's safety. If no family member is available, law enforcement may be called to check the welfare of the patient.

These arrangements are made with the patient in advance, either at the time of admission or during treatment if the patient's risk level changes.

**Figure 5.2** **SAMPLE EMERGENCY INFORMATION WALLET CARD**

## BMC Crisis Card

*In a crisis, call 911 or*
*go to the nearest emergency room.*

Suicide Prevention Lifeline **1-800-273-TALK**(8255)
TTY Number **1-800-799-4TTY**(4889)

Alternatives to Domestic Violence **1-800-339-7233**

Child Abuse Hotline **1-800-827-8724**

Community Crisis Hotline **1-800-603-4673**

Youth Crisis Hotline **1-800-448-4683**

---

Other contact information:

_____

_____

_____

_____

 **LOMA LINDA UNIVERSITY BEHAVIORAL MEDICINE CENTER**
1710 Barton Road
Redlands, CA 92373
Non-emergency number 909-558-9275

LLUMCMKTG#BMC-041-06/1206/2000

Source: LLUBMC. Used with permission

# Communication with family/caregivers

With a patient at risk for suicide, communication with family/caregivers is essential to patient safety. In some cases, this need for family involvement may create Health Insurance Portability and Accountability Act (HIPAA) issues and conflicts. Obviously, each facility must grapple with these conflicts when providing policies and training regarding HIPAA issues and communication with family members. These are not easy decisions, and different facilities may take different approaches. Patient's Rights, Patient Care, and Information Management committees should address these policies, depending on the structure of these committees. Some facilities may have a dedicated HIPAA office or staff to assist.

Some treatment philosophies hold that the patient's right to decide whether to involve family members is absolute. Others may choose to retain an option to override this right in order to protect the patient in certain situations. It can be a political, cultural, ethical, and legal minefield. Therefore, access to an ethical and/or legal consultant is extremely valuable in situations where a patient objects to disclosing confidential information to family members. Obviously, every effort should be made to work with and encourage the patient to allow the involvement of family or caregivers.

**Social support structures are absolutely essential for the suicidal patient.**
If no support system exists, one must be developed prior to discharge. Ideally, there is someone who can be designated to be available for the patient and

involved in discharge planning and emergency contingencies. These can include family, friends, neighbors, church members, or individuals from the community who volunteer to provide support. Lacking this, coordination of care and communication with community agencies providing treatment are essential, along with crisis referrals.

Prior to discharge from a 24-hour setting and following treatment for a suicide attempt, a family meeting including the patient, family members or significant others, and clinical staff is strongly recommended. The American Association of Suicidology (AAS) recommends that this meeting cover the following topics:

- The warning signs of suicide

- The increased risk for suicide during the scheduled time to leave a program or following discharge

- The need for the patient to adhere to medication and other treatment regimens

- An explanation of how psychiatric symptoms may impair judgment

- Emphasis on the need for the patient to avoid use of intoxicants and how intoxicants can increase suicide risk

- The need for the removal of the means for suicide as much as possible

- Education about the risk associated with firearms [3]

The first month after discharge from 24-hour care is a time of elevated risk: 50 percent of post-discharge suicides happen in the first week following discharge.[4] Careful planning during this time should involve family and caregivers to minimize these risks. In addition to the information listed by AAS, family members should be given detailed information about how to access help for the patient, including 24-hour emergency hotline numbers and phone numbers to reach the treating clinicians providing follow-up care. These instructions should be given both verbally and in writing.

## Communication and medical records

In looking at root cause analyses (RCAs) of patient suicides, lapses in communication and in patient assessment and reassessment were among the top recurring issues from 1995 to 2005.[5] Both of these root causes may be the result of incomplete, missing, or ineffective documentation.

Like the other NPSGs, the suicide risk assessment goal mandates communication through documentation to some extent, although it is up to each facility to determine how they document their compliance with the goal. The easiest method would be to have an initial screening tool, similar to the one developed by LLUBMC, for use as a part of the routine intake assessment packet (see

**Figure 4.1** in Chapter 4). If the screen indicates that the patient is not at significant risk at the time of assessment, this result should be noted.

For patients whose screening indicates further action may be necessary, the intervention or action should be documented in the progress notes and added to the treatment plan.

Reassessments, when indicated by the patient's condition or when planning for discharge, should also be documented. Often the same assessment form or screening tool can be used at different points during treatment and compared with earlier assessments.

> **TIP** Although no clinician can predict the future behavior of a patient, and no outcomes can ever be guaranteed, careful and thorough documentation can increase the coordination of care and decrease the risks inherent in treating the patient.

Assessment information that notes factors that decrease the suicide risk (e.g., strong family support, patient motivation, access and involvement with treatment, etc.) should also be included.

A usual first action in many settings may be to order a consultation with a psychiatrist, psychiatric emergency team (PET), or other mental health professional. Contact with that person, the time frame for response, and any interim precautions taken should be noted in the medical record. When the consultation is complete, the results should be documented as well, along with any treatment recommendations and orders.

Patients found to be at high risk are often placed on one-to-one observation. If a one-to-one staff member is not immediately available, interim safety measures that address the patient's immediate safety needs should be noted. There should be a tool used by one-to-one staff to document the patient's location, condition, affect, statements related to suicide, visitors, treatments, and responses at regular intervals (see **Figure 5.3**). Hand-off communication between one-to-one staff members should be both verbal and in writing at the change of each shift.

Environmental precautions recommended and taken should also be noted in the progress notes and treatment plan (e.g. "Removed cords from pajamas, shoelaces, and belt" or "Dietary order reflects that patient is to receive plastic utensils and no knives, staff to count utensils after each meal"). Medication needs and communication among nurses should also reflect any precautions and compliance issues.

A preprinted sheet of precautions can be developed particular to the treatment setting, with the appropriate items checked. (A sample precaution sheet appears in Chapter 8.)

| Figure 5.3 | **SAMPLE DISCHARGE/TRANSITION-OF-CARE PLAN** |

Patient name: _____

Expected course of recovery (to extent known):
___ Not known at this time          ___ Other: _____

Medications to be taken at home: _____

**NOTE:** Refer to the Home Medication List for all medications to be taken at home. Do not take any medications that are not listed unless you are instructed to do so by your primary care physician.

Recommended follow-up
Physician: _____ Therapist: _____
Address: _____ Address: _____
Telephone: _____ Telephone: _____
___ Patient will call for an appointment
___ Patient will call for an appointment
          within ___ days.          within ___ days.

Other referrals/recommendations:
___ Follow-up lab/test          ___ See primary care physician for
___ Support group               ___ Occupation/education
___ Support group               ___ Activity/recreation
___ 12 step                     ___ Other

Notes:
_____
_____
_____
_____

| Figure 5.3 | **SAMPLE DISCHARGE/TRANSITION-OF-CARE PLAN (CONT.)** |
|---|---|

Additional instructions

Discharge residence: _____

Estimated date of return to work or school: _____

Diet: _____

Other: _____

If your symptoms worsen or you are in crisis, call 911 or go to the nearest emergency room.
You may also call the following hotlines:

    (800) 273-TALK

    Child Abuse Hotline: _____

    Community Crisis Hotline: _____

    Youth Crisis Hotline: _____

Your personal support is: _____

Name and address of the family member or other person whil may receive a copy of this plan:

_____

    __ Accepted copy               __ Declined copy

I have read and understand this discharge plan._____

Patient: _____ Date: _____

Guardian: _____ Date: _____

Staff member signature: _____ Date: _____

*Source: LLUBMC. Adapted and reprinted with permission.*

When releasing, discharging, transferring, or transitioning a patient to a higher or lower level of care, rationale for these treatment decisions should be documented. Patient and family meetings and instructions, particularly instructions for discharge, should be documented as well. Depending on the setting, discharge paperwork can be preprinted with 24-hour emergency information. Specific precautions and recommendations must be noted in the medical record and copies of information given to patients and caregivers should be placed in the medical record.

Hand-off communication within the treatment setting, with other levels of care within the organization, and with outside individuals or agencies to whom the patient is being referred, should be completed according to organizational policy and Joint Commission and HIPAA regulations.

## Supporting policies and documentation

Policies and procedures regarding the assessment and reassessment of patients should match the standards of practice and regulations appropriate for each treatment setting. Criteria for admission, discharge, and transitions to other levels of care should be outlined in the policy. Treatment practices regarding safety precautions should be reflected in hospital policies and/or guidelines.

Specific training provided to staff should be outlined in policy and documented in personnel files as required. Records of attendance at training modules or employee orientation, and completion of required competencies related to

# STAFF NUMBER, SKILL MIX, AND TRAINING

Staff requirements, a perennial issue at hospitals nationwide, are particularly important to effective suicide assessment and prevention. This facet of suicide-risk assessment is addressed in the second Implementation Expectation (IE) of the NPSG, regarding appropriate patient care and setting; and in the *Comprehensive Accreditation Manual for Hospitals (CAMH)* standard HR.1.10 (adequate number/mix of staff).

The issues of staff number and skill mix necessary to address suicidal risk effectively in any particular setting are complex, and each organization must determine the best solutions based on their staff levels and the patient population they serve. Challenges include

- the changing needs of the patient

- the unpredictable influx of such patients to hospital emergency departments and psychiatric hospitals

- environmental and training issues faced by each setting

It's a balancing act for any facility, even in the best of circumstances.

The Joint Commission's analysis of inpatient suicide shows staffing issues to be a relatively minor contributor to the root causes of suicide (eighth out of 12 measures from 1995–2004 and 10th of 12 in 2005[1]), possibly because it is difficult to directly correlate staffing issues to patient outcomes.

However, adequate staffing is already a major issue in many systems, and is an essential component of the suicide risk-and-prevention equation. In cases where inadequate staffing results in a publicized incident—such as when a suicidal patient manages to elude staff long enough to harm himself or herself—the issue of staffing can cause heated debate among line staff and administration, outcry from the public, and scrutiny from regulatory agencies.

In this chapter, we will explore the elements in determining appropriate staffing levels, variety of skills, and necessary training.

## Environmental factors and staffing needs

For facilities developing a comprehensive suicide risk–assessment and prevention policy for the first time, a good first step is an assessment of environmental factors in the treatment settings. Most hospitals have not been specifically designed to mitigate the risk of self-harm, and may be teeming with potential hazards—from a lack of ED safe rooms near nursing stations to doors that can be jammed shut and bathroom fixtures that can be used for hanging. An area with many potential hazards will very likely require more staff monitoring and intervention. (See the case study in Chapter 8 for more about environmental assessments.)

For hospitals or departments that have patient areas designed with the suicidal patient's safety in mind, less direct-staff supervision might be acceptable in some situations. However, no environment is foolproof, and a room with minimal hazards can never take the place of vigilant staff monitoring. Environmental design can certainly make the job easier, though.

## One-to-one monitoring and support

Once a patient has been determined to be at significant risk for self-harm, a common and effective intervention is to place the patient on one-to-one monitoring until the risk has diminished or until the patient can be transferred to a higher level of care or to another facility. Various staff members are used in different settings to perform this role. Some emergency departments use security staff while others use nursing assistants, or registry "sitters."

Regardless of the type of staff used, your facility must implement specific training to make sure that the designated staff member is aware of potential hazards and the importance of constant vigilance. Specific training should be included in a hospital's written policies, and training and competence documented in personnel records.

A staff member providing one-to-one supervision must maintain visual contact with the patient at all times. This requires that staff members

- have no other duties during this time

- be relieved by another staff member for breaks or when errands are needed for the patient

- be alert at all times

- be prevented from dozing off during the night

As this list indicates, personnel with one-to-one duties will require support from
other staff. At LLUBMC, for example, staff members often switch off duty for
one-to-one supervision, sometimes at two- or four-hour intervals. Support staff
check on the one-to-one staff often and offer relief or breaks when needed.

## Availability of psychiatric staff

For inpatient psychiatric facilities, it's standard practice to have a psychiatrist,
psychologist, or other licensed clinician available to provide more in-depth suicide risk assessments, and such specialists are easily accessible in most cases.
However, ready access to psychiatric staff can be more challenging for non-
behavioral EDs as well as other behavioral health settings, including residential
programs, chemical dependency programs, and outpatient clinics.

For nonpsychiatric settings, it will be extremely valuable to have a formal relationship with mental-health professionals who can further assess the patient

when indicated. They also would be helpful in consulting with hospital leadership regarding policies and procedures to minimize risks, and reviewing staff training materials.

In some areas, Crisis Response Teams (CRTs) are available through the state department of mental health. There may also be psychiatric emergency teams (PETs) or consultation and liaison teams that are associated with local psychiatric facilities and can respond to emergency rooms or other settings to provide patient evaluations. Where no psychiatric consultation is available and the patient has been deemed to be at risk, efforts should be made to transfer the patient to a mental health–assessment center, county-designated setting, or private psychiatric facility for further evaluation as soon as possible.

When the patient cannot be transferred because of medical necessity or bed availability, hospitals must outline their contingency plans to address patients' psychiatric and assessment needs until the patient can be moved to the appropriate level of care.

## Consulting staff

Because of the challenges of maintaining adequate availability of psychiatrists or other licensed mental-health professionals, it is helpful to have psychiatric consultation available. Policies should address the use of consulting staff and outline how the competence of these staff members is monitored. (The *CAMH* requires hospitals to have credentialing procedures for community physicians who have privileges at the hospital. The professionals' credentials are periodically reviewed to ensure competence. These procedures and processes should include mental-health professionals.)

In addition, for facilities that don't have in-house legal and ethical resources, external consultation can be helpful when addressing the issues associated with managing suicidal patients.

## Contract staff, travelers, floaters, and sitters

Because of the unpredictable and immediate staffing needs created by potentially suicidal patients, it is often necessary to rely on registry staff or available staff from other departments, at least temporarily. When utilizing ancillary staff members, it is important to ensure that they are competent to provide services to the patient and have received the necessary training to recognize high-risk situations, indicators of suicidal risk, emergency procedures, and that they have an understanding of the safety issues and level of supervision necessary to protect the patient.

Most often, these are not regular staff members and may be unfamiliar with the unit and the patient. They should be oriented to relevant unit procedures and briefed on the specific needs of the patient they are assigned to monitor prior to beginning care.

## Training and competence

Joint Commission statistics list staff orientation and training as the third-highest root cause for inpatient suicides from 1995 to 2004, and the fourth-highest root cause in 2005.[2] All staff members who will encounter and provide care for possibly suicidal patients need specific training to recognize high-risk factors, control environmental risks, and understand treatment issues related to suicide prevention and intervention. The focus of training and degree of training needed will depend upon the role of the staff in the treatment of the patient.

Basic training entails

- how to recognize a suicidal patient

- how to recognize environmental safety factors

- communication and documentation requirements, including
    - immediate steps to take to protect the patient's safety.
    - how to notify the right person when suicidal comments or behaviors are observed
    - the related documentation required

Part of new-employee orientation should include information about environmental risks, because minimizing these risks encompasses most, if not all, departments of the hospital.

Orientation should include staff from

- housekeeping
- pharmacy
- security
- dietary staff
- maintenance
- nursing

For direct caregivers, additional training should be provided that focuses on

■ assessment
■ interviewing skills
■ recognition of risks
■ discharge planning
■ documentation

Training should also address awareness of staff attitudes toward suicide and suicidal patients. The goal of attitude awareness is to improve patient care by increasing staff empathy for and understanding of the dynamics of the suicidal patient.

Specific competencies may be indicated for clinical staff regarding

- knowledge of the hospital's assessment tools
- interviewing skills
- suicide risk factors
- preventing access to dangerous materials
- treatment planning
- safety precautions
- community resources

Staff members who provide one-to-one monitoring of suicidal patients should be able to demonstrate competence of the skills needed for such monitoring. Competence and training should be reflected in the employee's personnel file; **Figure 6.1** shows how one-to-one competence can be documented.

> **TIP**
> One-to-one competency could be a tracer activity for a suicidal patient. Conduct a mock tracer to gauge staff preparedness for surveyor questions about one-to-one care and other program-specific issues. (See Chapter 9 for more about the suicide prevention tracer.)

As with patient assessment and treatment measures, hospitals can look to psychiatric facilities for guidance. LLUBMC and others provide training on basic suicide assessment for all employees at new employee orientation and include environmental safety on nursing staff first-day orientation checklists.

| Figure 6.1 | SAMPLE ONE-TO-ONE COMPETENCY CHECKLIST FOR STAFF |
|---|---|

*Loma Linda University Behavioral Medicine Center*

**STAFF COMPETENCY CHECKLIST**

*1:1 OBSERVATION PROCEDURES*

Employee Name: _____     Date: _____

| Demonstrates skills and knowledge essential to provide competent care or service for providing 1:1 observations. | Performed correctly and independently *(indicated by reviewer's initials)* |
|---|---|
| • Describe the 1:1 level of observation:<br> ❖ Staff member's positioning in relation to the patient<br> ❖ Procedure for initiating 1:1 observation (licensed staff)<br> ❖ Physician order—initial and renewal (licensed staff)<br> ❖ Patient use of sharps during 1:1<br> ❖ Patient use of bathroom during 1:1<br> ❖ Other important considerations for ensuring patient safety | |
| • List clinical indications for placing a patient on 1:1 level of observation | |
| • List documentation requirements for a patient on 1:1 level of observation<br> ❖ Physician's Order Sheet<br> ❖ Progress Note<br> ❖ Patient Observation Sheet<br> ❖ Treatment Plan | |
| • List information a staff member should have prior to accepting responsibility for a patient on 1:1 level of observation | |
| • List two examples of behaviors that would indicate an increase in the risk level of the patient | |
| • Describe interventions you may use to address the above identified behaviors | |

Reviewer's Signature: _____     Initial: _____

Required competency for the following positions/departments as indicated by check box:

❑ R.N.      ❑ L.V.N.      ❑ L.P.T.      ❑ B.H.S.     ❑ Other: _____

*Source: LLUBMC. Reprinted with permission.*

Annual online orientation also covers this content and is completed yearly by all staff. Additional competency training is provided for social workers, therapists, and psychologists on suicide assessment and interventions. Unit staff also have specific competency training on one-to-one observation, interviewing, and contraband checks.

**TIP** Your time and your staff's time is valuable. If you're having trouble determining a workable balance of staff, skills, and training, contact a behavioral health center in your area, or your state department of mental health.

## Summary

Determining and maintaining a working balance of staff members with appropriate skills is challenging, to say the least. Although staff level and mix is not a leading root cause of patient suicide, according to Joint Commission statistics, having the right balance is a necessity when caring for patients at risk of harming themselves.

Hospital departments must work together to ensure

- that both in-house staff and contracted service employees are knowledgeable about issues such as one-to-one monitoring
- that education programs are available
- and that staff education is documented.

Hospitals that are creating a suicide risk assessment policy for the first time should look to behavioral facilities for some guidance regarding employee knowledge and staff mix.

## Endnotes

1. The Joint Commission, "Root Causes of Inpatient Suicides, 1995-2004," and "Root Causes of Inpatient Suicides, 2005," *www.jointcommission.org/NR/rdonlyres/1A0D7C31-2BF2-4D6C-B415-B1C27E2075ED/0/se_rc_inpatient_suicides.jpg.* Accessed December 2006.

2. Ibid.

# CHAPTER SEVEN

## BETTER ASSESSMENT VIA FMEA

# CHAPTER SEVEN

# BETTER ASSESSMENT VIA FMEA

The Joint Commission requires that healthcare facilities conduct failure modes and effects analyses (FMEA) to proactively address patient safety issues.[1] This kind of organizationwide analysis has proven very effective at improving quality and systems in other industries, and can be very useful for pinpointing trouble spots in health care processes as well.

Reducing the risk of patient suicide is a good candidate for this type of analysis, because the process of minimizing risks can begin when the patient walks through the door. Recognizing patients who are at higher risk for suicide will set the stage for everything that follows, and an FMEA can help your facility locate and reduce risks that patients might encounter from admission to discharge.

As previous chapters have discussed, your facility's initial screen for suicide risk and subsequent assessments help all staff recognize and respond quickly to protect potentially suicidal patients. In this chapter, we will examine how conducting an FMEA can reduce the risk of patient suicide rates in your facility, while demonstrating compliance with the suicide risk assessment NPSG.

LLUBMC conducted a failure modes and effects analysis to determine our risk for patient suicide and to take preventative action. We completed the suicide prevention FMEA in 2005, and used our findings to strengthen patient care throughout the facility. Although the FMEA process required significant investments of time, staff, and energy, the net result—safer patients and more knowledgeable staff—was worth the effort. **Figure 7.1** shows the steps involved in our FMEA process.

1. **Teamwork.** We began by organizing our FMEA team. We had the support of hospital management from the beginning, because they understood how serious a threat patient suicide can be. We made an effort to include staff from all areas of the hospital, including

   - nurse managers from each unit and outpatient program managers
   - a representative from social services
   - an attending physician representative

Other hospital committees were involved at different points of the project, including human resources, patient care, environment of care, and information management personnel.

2. **Brainstorming opportunities for harm.** Our next step was an attempt to discover all the possible ways that a patient could harm himself or herself. We reviewed patient files and considered the "close calls" and attempts that we'd had in our facility, along with incidents at

| Figure 7.1 | **LLUBMC's FMEA PROCESS STEP BY STEP** |

1. Assemble team, including leadership and all levels of staff

2. Develop process flow for process under analysis

3. Identify potential failure modes, based on everyone's input

4. Determine the worst potential adverse consequence (patient suicide)

5. Determine contributory factors for each failure mode

6. Redesign the process to minimize the risk to patients

7. Test, implement, and monitor the redesigned process

nearby facilities, Joint Commission sentinel event reports, and a review of literature regarding inpatient suicide.

3. **Areas for assessment.** From our initial brainstorming sessions, we developed a list of key areas to assess that included

- environmental risks
- patient assessment and reassessment
- staff education
- documentation
- patient education
- discharge planning

For environmental risks, each manager conducted a tour of his or her unit with key staff, and the environment-of-care team performed a hospitalwide assessment.

4. **Recommendations.** From there, the environment-of-care committee developed a list of environmental hazards and recommendations. The recommendations included

- changing door handles and hinges
- removing grab bars from most patient rooms
- removing closet poles
- eliminating plastic trash can liners and plastic patient-belonging bags

(See Chapter 8 for more on environmental assessment.)

The patient-care committee suggested that patient gowns with ties be eliminated or the ties be shortened. We eventually opted for snap closures on patient gowns.

Nurse managers asked their staff to review the lists of contraband and recommend any additions or improvements. Although the staff considered the lists to be satisfactory, the nurse managers and staff determined that staff training could be improved, so a competency on patient contraband checks was developed and implemented to ensure that all staff members were well trained on checking for contraband and securing or eliminating hazardous items.

In addition, the nurse managers also reviewed the procedures and training for staff doing one-to-one monitoring of suicidal patients. They recommended and developed a competency to ensure that all staff members assigned to one-to-one monitoring of suicidal patients are proficient at recognizing high-risk behaviors and situations, and monitoring patients to minimize suicidal risks.

The outpatient departments suggested that all key clinicians have a standard voicemail message that specifically gives crisis information to any patient who might call after hours in a crisis. They also revised the information given to patients at intake to make sure patients are educated about what to do and who to call if they feel suicidal outside of program hours. This information was also included on the discharge plan for all inpatient programs.

The patient-care committee looked at patient assessment and reassessment forms and procedures. Although most of the information regarding risk factors (identified during the literature review) was present, the information wasn't pulled together in a specific suicide-risk screen. The committee developed a screen and then presented it to the medical staff and research team for suggestions and approval.

The forms were then sent to the information-management committee and incorporated into the patient-assessment and reassessment process. Patient-assessment policies and procedure were adjusted to reflect the new suicide screen and discharge plans. The human resources committee then developed and implemented staff education regarding suicide-risk factors and assessment. Employee orientation materials regarding suicide risks were reviewed and updated as well.

Although the FMEA took time and required input from all areas of the hospital, it showed everyone from leadership to line staff exactly where we needed to improve our precautions against patient suicide. This made it easier to create and implement our suicide-risk assessment and prevention strategies. **Figures 7.2** and **7.3** show our FMEA process and recommendations. Other healthcare settings can adapt these processes to conduct an FMEA that's most effective for their environment.

The case study at the end of this chapter provides more tips and strategies for FMEA success. Additional resources include the Joint Commission Web site, and FMEA-focused publications.[2]

An FMEA should assess your entire system and help you answer questions like these:

- Can staff recognize possible warning signs of a suicidal patient?

- Do they know when to screen a patient for suicide risk?

- Is your initial screen effective in identifying patients at risk?

- Does your policy include a place for written documentation of staff suicide-awareness training?

- Are patient treatment areas as safe as they can be?

- Have you developed a policy to check patient-care areas for items that can induce risk, and to instruct staff to remove them?

## SAMPLE **FMEA** FOR PATIENT SUICIDE ASSESSMENT AND PREVENTION

Figure 7.2

**Topic Status**—Suicide is the primary cause of death among psychiatric inpatients.

**Project selection** —Each year the hospital identifies one such high-risk process on which to conduct a failure modes and effects analysis (FMEA) to proactively address patient safety, risk reduction, and loss prevention.

**Observations**—Specific risk-screening-and-prevention guidelines vary from unit to unit and program to program

- Formal documentation and protocol for outpatients who may become suicidal outside of regular program hours is lacking

- Current practices—Current suicide risk assessments are conducted for all patients on the nursing assessment and the psychiatric evaluation

Ongoing daily assessment of suicidal ideation/risk is documented by physicians and nursing staff for inpatient psychiatric units

Inpatient units have suicide prevention safety contracts available, but their use varies from unit to unit

Need for increased monitoring of patients at high risk for suicide is determined by acuity-level assignments and in individual treatment plans

All employees receive training on suicide risk assessment during orientation

The adult PHP program uses safety contracts routinely

Youth services IOP programs currently handle patients at risk for suicide on an individual basis and do not routinely use formal suicide risk assessments or safety contracts

| Figure 7.2 | **SAMPLE FMEA FOR PATIENT SUICIDE ASSESSMENT AND PREVENTION (CONT.)** |
|---|---|

No formal documentation instructs patients admitted to outpatient programs on how to handle psychiatric emergencies occurring outside of program hours—although clinicians do discuss this with patients at intake

Discharge aftercare plans do not clearly state what patients should do if experiencing a psychiatric emergency before their first scheduled outpatient appointment [end list]

**Proposed practices**—Develop standardized phone-message protocol that gives emergency information for outpatient therapists to use

- Develop uniform safety contracts and guidelines for their use for inpatient and outpatient programs

- Add contact information to aftercare plans for psychiatric emergencies

- Review suicide assessment orientation materials

**Training**—Provide training on policy and procedure to charge nurses, clinical therapists, intake, and house supervisors

- Review orientation materials' coverage of suicide assessment and risk management

**Implementation**—Documentation reviewed and approved through information management, provision of care, and behavioral healthcare committees

- Revised forms distributed to units

- Training presented at staff meetings (regarding safety contracts, phone messages, aftercare planning)

**Ongoing monitoring**—24-hour chart checklist of treatment plans and safety contracts

*Source: LLUBMC. Reprinted with permission.*

| Figure 7.3 | **SAMPLE FMEA-BASED PLAN OF ACTION** |
|---|---|

| Current practice | Observations | Action items | Next steps |
|---|---|---|---|
| Suicide risk is assessed on the nursing assessment and psychiatric evaluation | Specific risk screening and prevention guidelines vary among units and programs | Develop suicide risk screen for assessment and reassessment (complete, given to PC team) | Integrate new content into forms<br><br>Random chart audit for completion of new screens |
| Ongoing assessment is documented by MD and RN, or therapist for OP, in daily/weekly progress notes and in the treatment plan | Assessment information varied from person to person | Develop more detailed training for masters-level outpatient clinicians | Introduce new forms, assessment tools, safety contracts, and phone protocols in staff meetings and/or in-service training |
| Acuity levels for increased monitoring of patients at risk are assessed each shift and adjusted as required | Staff providing 1:1 observation could benefit from additional training on ongoing monitoring of suicide risks | Develop 1:1 competency to assess staff ability to monitor and assess high risk patients (referred to PC team) | Provide training and complete new competencies for 1:1 |
| All employees receive training on suicide risk assessment during orientation | | Review suicide assessment orientation materials<br><br>•Develop contraband competency to reduce risk of patient accessing hazardous items (referred to PC team) | Provide training and complete new competencies for contraband |
| Annual environmental safety audits target environmental safety related to suicide and self harm risk, quarterly audits may not be specific for potential self-harm risks | Routine EC audits may not specifically target potential environmental risks for suicide and self-harm. | Review/assess environmental risk factors for suicide and self-harm (referred to EC team)<br><br>•Develop contraband competency to reduce risk of patient accessing hazardous items (referred to PC team) | Follow-up on recommendations from EC team<br><br>Provide training and complete new competencies for contraband<br><br>Track incidents of self-harm via incident reporting and RCA process to identify and respond to additional identified areas of risk |
| There is no standard documentation about instructing outpatients during the admission process on how to handle after-hours psychiatric emergencies | Formal documentation and protocol for outpatients who become suicidal outside of program hours is lacking | Develop standardized phone message protocol for outpatient therapists that give emergency instructions<br><br>Create emergency cards that all patients receive (at admission for outpatients, and at discharge for inpatients) | Ongoing tracking of incidents of self-harm through incident reporting & RCA process to identity and respond to any additional identified areas of risk |
| Discharge aftercare plans do not clearly state how patients should handle psychiatric emergencies arising after discharge | Documentation of discharge information provided to patients regarding crisis management is not standardized | •Add hotline numbers and emergency instructions to aftercare plan | Ongoing tracking of after-care-plan information |

*Complied from information supplied by LLUBMC. Reprinted with permission.*

## Case Study: Wayne Memorial Hospital, Goldsboro, NC

With changes in North Carolina's mental-health laws looming, a keen awareness of The Joint Commission's sentinel events data, and the impending arrival of the suicide risk assessment goal, the Organizational Performance Improvement and Patient Safety team at Wayne Memorial Hospital, in Goldsboro, NC, decided the time was right to conduct an FMEA on patient suicide assessment and prevention.

"We felt like we had to do it for patient safety," says Barbara Lewis Shelton, MBA-HCM, RNC, director of Organizational Performance Improvement and Patient Safety at the 316-bed, nonprofit general medical facility. The analysis yielded changes that led to more accurate patient suicide risk assessments, more frequent reassessments, and greater staff awareness of patient suicide risk and prevention, she says.

Mental-health reform measures in the state are closing some facilities, and will have a "major effect on the ER," as well as a projected increase in med/surg cases, Shelton says. Wayne Memorial has a voluntary inpatient psychiatric unit, but suicidal patients will have to be admitted to the ICU for one-to-one care, "and that's not a long-term option," given the hospital's demand for critical-care beds, says Shelton.

The hospital decided to conduct an FMEA to look at all areas that would be affected by patients at risk for suicide, and to fine-tune suicide risk assessment and prevention policies. Shelton says the hospital's leadership was supportive from the very beginning of the process, when she submitted a recommendation to conduct the FMEA. They, too, were very concerned about the Sentinel Event Data and aware of what could happen if the ED began to treat more psychiatric patients, she says.

The Performance Improvement team began by enlisting help from

- the behavioral health department
- the psychiatric social worker
- clinical resource management
- the administrative director of critical care
- the director of the ICU
- representatives from Med/Surg unit
- ED staff

Team members conducted assessments of all areas of care, and studied the process from when the patient enters the facility to discharge. This thorough survey yielded several areas for improvement.

For example, "the Nurse Admission Assessment needed to change" to include "trigger questions" such as whether the patient has a history of mental illness, history of depression, and whether the patient is thinking of killing himself or herself, says Shelton.

Patient reassessments were also revised to include questioning the patient if they were feeling depressed, helpless or hopeless to a once-a-shift schedule. This would enable the nursing staff to make appropriate changes to implement precautions until a psychiatric consult could be completed or until it was determined by the physician that the patient was not a danger to him/herself or others.

The FMEA team's recommendations were submitted early in 2007.

Shelton has the following advice for hospitals conducting an FMEA on patient suicide:

■ **Be prepared to invest a lot of time and effort in the FMEA process.** Building a team, assigning duties, and assessing an entire facility are daunting tasks.

■ **Don't re-create the wheel.** Plenty of other facilities are analyzing their suicide assessment and prevention policies—"use templates others have created, and make them your own," she says.

■ **Get the right players on your team at the beginning.** This can help you avoid investing time and effort in the project, only to discover things need to be redone because a vital area of care or a key piece of the process was left out.

■ **Get executive support.** Given the higher level of attention that patient suicide is now generating, the NPSG requirements, and sentinel event data, most hospital leaders will be receptive to the project. Get their buy-in early with a formal recommendation for the FMEA, and include them in the process as well as the final submission.

## Summary

Used for years in other industries to improve systems and eliminate problems, the FMEA process can help you identify your facility's strengths and weaknesses relative to protecting suicidal patients. Although an FMEA requires a system-wide investment of time and resources, the results can clearly show where your systems and policies are working, and where there is room for improvement.

An effective FMEA can also help you prioritize any required improvements, and provides documentation that will help you demonstrate compliance with The Joint Commission's NPSG for suicide risk assessment.

## Endnotes

1. The Joint Commission, *Reducing risk of patient suicide*, © 2005, JCR Inc.

2. A variety of resources are available to help facilities with the FMEA process. Among these are "Failure Modes and Effects Analysis: Building Safety into Everyday Practice," by Glenn D. Krasker, MHSA. ©2004, HCPro, Inc.

# BUILDING A SAFE ENVIRONMENT

# BUILDING A SAFE ENVIRONMENT

Your facility tries to take every possible safety precaution. But every once in a while, somehow, a patient manages to get hold of something they shouldn't, and you have "a learning experience" on your hands. Although the results are usually inconsequential or minor for the patient, these incidents are troubling reminders that no facility is risk-free.

The goal of environmental safety is to prevent that event from happening in the first place by constantly monitoring the environment of care and evaluating strategies for improvement. The suicide risk assessment NPSG calls on organizations to conduct proactive risk assessments that evaluate the potential adverse impact of healthcare buildings, grounds, equipment, occupants, and internal physical systems on the safety of patients, staff, and others coming to the facility.

Furthermore, every organization must use the risks identified to select and implement procedures and controls to achieve the lowest potential for adverse impact on the safety and health of patients, staff, and other people coming to the organization's facilities.[1]

Unless you're starting from scratch and are designing a new facility, it's likely that all desired improvements can't take place immediately. Therefore, a good place to start is an in-depth environmental scan that specifically targets potential problem areas for suicidal patients. This will require a different examination than the usual check for fall hazards, worn carpet, exposed light bulbs, and such. (See **Figure 8.1**)

## Recruiting an environmental risk team

During the environmental scan, a team of people from different departments in your facility will periodically take a tour of the area where psychiatric patients are seen. This team will scrutinize the area from top to bottom for hazards, trying to look at their surroundings through the eyes of a potentially suicidal patient.

 **TIP**  No fixture, window, or room can be made suicide-proof. The purpose of an environmental assessment is to identify and reduce potential risk as much as possible.

As you evaluate your care environment, encourage people from various medical and nonmedical disciplines to join the environmental assessment team. Participants could include personnel who might deal with potentially suicidal patients, such as

---

| Figure 8.1 | **SAMPLE PHYSICAL ENVIRONMENT RISK ASSESSMENT** |

*LOMA LINDA UNIVERSTIY BEHAVIORAL MEDICINE CENTER*

**Scoring:**     0 = no risk     1 = some risk     2 = moderate risk     3 = considerable risk

|  | Internal Incidents In past 15 years | Community Incidents | Patients Voicing Intent to Harm using these Items | **Total Score** |
|---|---|---|---|---|
| Bathroom doors * a | 1 | 1 | 0 | **2** |
| Exposed toilet and sink plumbing *b | 0 | 1 | 0 | **1** |
| Closet door hinges *c | 0 | 1 | 0 | **1** |
| Electric beds | 0 | 1 | 0 | **1** |
| Window coverings | 0 | 0 | 0 | **0** |
| Shower control handles | 0 | 0 | 0 | **0** |

**Summary:**

The BMC nursing staff makes rounds on the psychiatric services every 15 minutes around the clock. If any patient is deemed at greater risk for self-harm, he or she is placed on Level 4 acuity or up to a 1:1 constant observation. This may account for only one incident in the past 15 years. As we look to pursue greater safety of our environment, the next step is to consider replacing the bathroom door handles with ones to which nothing can be tied.

**Actions taken:**

        2005   Hospital gown for all transfers from LLUMC ED
        2005   Hospital gown for all new admits
        2005   Pre-assessment search process
        2005   Bathroom door handles changed out
        2005   Bathroom light fixtures replaced with unbreakable covers
        1999   Curtains replaced with break-away pull-down shades
        1995   Fire sprinkler heads recessed with break-away heads
        1991   Showerheads replaced with flat model

**Recommendations:**

*a Bathroom door handles were changed out on patient care units
*b Estimates for enclosing plumbing feasibility (cost and functionality)
*c Door hinges need to be either removed or moved so they are exposed in the corridor

*Source: LLUBMC. Used with permission.*

- maintenance staff

- nursing

- dietary

- housekeeping

- physician

- other key staff—for example, receptionists or security personnel could be included if they are involved in screening visitors

Recruiting representatives from these groups is easy if most of them are already on your facility's Environment of Care (EOC) committee. If not, a quarterly invitation may pull some of these staff members into the mix. Although department managers can perform this scan, it is invaluable to have front-line staff input. In larger facilities, it might make more sense to identify smaller ad hoc teams within each department to scan their work areas and report back to the EOC committee.

## Scanning the facility

At LLUBMC, staff from each unit does a monthly "environment of care round" and submits a report to the EOC committee. A more in-depth, annual scan is done by the EOC committee chair, the director of nurses, the director of building and safety, and each unit's managers.

From your building tour and a review of patient procedures (how contraband items are handled, what visitors are allowed and when, etc.) the environmental assessment group should come up with a "hit list" of things to be changed, purchased, eliminated, or moved. It is also helpful to gather information from root cause analyses (RCAs) at the facility, or to collect data about specific patient incidents that have occurred.

A review of Joint Commission sentinel event RCAs is a good idea as well. Information and forms are available at *www.jointcommission.org/SentinelEvents/.*

Once a list of action items has been developed, the items can be prioritized and target dates can be set for implementation. Some will be "easy fixes" while others, such as replacing plumbing or windows, or implementing metal-detecting procedures, will require considerable planning, expenses, or major changes in procedures. (See the case study at the end of this chapter.)

## Reducing hazards

Although LLUBMC was designed as a psychiatric facility and was built fairly recently, the setting still provides considerable environmental challenges. We tackled some of the smaller recommendations first, such as retooling our contraband lists, changing door hinges and shower heads to reduce the risk of hanging, and using paper trash-can liners and patient-belonging bags instead of plastic, to reduce the possibility that these bags could be used for suffocation.

One of the larger projects undertaken at LLUBMC was the replacement or addition of protective laminate to the existing windows, which we accomplished section by section.

Keep in mind that merely replacing potentially hazardous fixtures and other equipment isn't enough, as LLUBMC learned. On a recent environmental round on the children's unit, a psychiatrist noticed that the push-pull door handles that we had installed (at considerable expense) to eliminate attaching anything to them had been installed upside down so that the handle pointed up rather than down, creating a hook. We quickly did a check of other units, and discovered that all of the handles had been installed upside down.

Further investigation revealed that the upside-down installation had been done to prevent something from being tied around the handle then thrown over the door. Either way seemed to present a different hazard.

In addition to vigilance, communication—letting the workers know what the intent was in replacing the doors—is a vital element of patient safety.

## Patient belongings

Maintaining a safe environment for patients means keeping a close eye on what comes into the facility as well as identifying the potential hazards that are already there. A policy regarding personal belongings is an important aspect of safeguarding the environment. Therefore, once a patient has been identified as having an elevated risk for suicide, personal items that could be used for self-harm should be removed and either stored or sent home.

Certain "standard precautions" should be outlined that would apply to all at-risk patients, with adjustments made to be more or less stringent to meet the needs of the individual. This may require that the patient and his or her belongings be searched. Facilities should consider the patients' rights implications of this search and consult with the Patient's Rights Office of the county mental-health department, as well as hospital legal counsel, when developing policies and procedures regarding contraband searches.

On an inpatient psychiatric unit, the needs of all patients should be considered, because items brought onto the unit by one patient could be accessible to other patients. Policies and guidelines should address this issue. Some personal-care items can be stored for safety and made available for use with supervision. (See **Figure 8.2** for LLUBMC's personal belongings policy.)

## Hospital-supplied items

As with personal articles, certain items that are normally used in patient-care areas should be restricted in areas where at-risk patients are treated. Some of these items can be easily replaced with safer alternatives; other items can be brought in and out of patient-care areas as needed by staff. For psychiatric facilities, patients may have access to some of these items when they have privileges, for example, permission to leave the unit to go to the cafeteria or to activities.

| Figure 8.2 | **SAMPLE PRECAUTIONARY LIST FOR PATIENT BELONGINGS** |

If a patient is screened as a potential suicide risk, the following items should be controlled or removed:

- belts, shoelaces, and cords from clothing (sweatshirts, for example)

- razors of any kind

- any item that has glass (make-up containers, picture frames, etc)

- metal items such as staples, paper clips, spiral-bound notebooks, etc.

- personal electric appliances such as hair dryers.

- nail files, clippers, tweezers, etc.

- products that would be harmful if ingested, such as aerosols, perfume, deodorant, nail polish, etc.

- any other items that could be used as weapons or used to cut, choke, ingest, or asphyxiate

- lighters, matches, etc.

- flowers and plants, unless known to be non-toxic if ingested

This list has been developed by the LLUBMC over time and is evaluated periodically as new situations arise.

*Source: LLUBMC. Used with permission.*

Care should be taken to ensure that restricted items are not brought back to the unit. Items brought onto the unit by staff must be carefully monitored to prevent them from being left behind or taken by a patient. At LLUBMC, hospital-supplied items that are restricted from high-risk patients include

- plastic trash-can liners (replace with paper)

- plastic patient-belonging bags (replace with paper)

- patient gowns with strings long enough to wrap around the neck

- metal and glass dining utensils (plasticware can be substituted, but should be accounted for after the meal; Consider eliminating even plastic knives)

- metal hangers (plastic ones may also be dangerous for certain patients)

- all sharp items as well as sharps containers

In addition

- any chemical items that could be harmful if ingested should not be left in patient-care areas

- all electric appliances should be removed when not in use unless they are permanently installed

- bed linens should be monitored to avoid patient having access to multiple sheets at one time

## Personnel precautions

It's important that all employees, visitors, and others be included in a hospital's plans for minimizing risks for potentially suicidal patients.

**Visitors'** belongings should be secured prior to visiting the suicidal patient. No purses, backpacks, etc. should be brought to the patient's room.

**Nurses** should ensure that medications have been swallowed after each dose. Pills cannot be left for the patient to take later. Nurses should also be careful that sharps are not inadvertently left where a patient might gain access to them.

**Pharmacy staff** should dispense discharge medications in blister packs where possible when these medications would be potentially lethal in an overdose.

**Physicians** should consider the potential lethality of medications prescribed for suicidal patients.

**Maintenance workers** in and around a suicidal patient's room should monitor tools, chemicals, and work carts, keeping them in view at all times.

Maintenance staff should keep dangerous tools such as box cutters, saws, etc. either on their person or stored securely when not in use.

**Housekeeping staff** should keep their work carts in view and hazardous items secured when in and around a suicidal patient's room.

**All staff** should be vigilant about patient access to exits or windows, especially on all floors above ground level.

## Environmental and equipment design and recommendations

Any recommendations and considerations for building design and equipment modifications need to be considered with respect to local building and safety codes. Not all facilities will want to or be able to implement all of the recommendations listed. Each facility and each patient population will have unique characteristics and needs.

The goal is not to create policies that will lead to a completely suicide-proof facility: That isn't possible. As National Association of Psychiatric Health Systems (NAPHS) literature notes, "No built environment—no matter how well designed and constructed—can be relied upon as an absolute preventative measure. Staff awareness of their environment, the latent risks of that environment, and the behavioral characteristics and needs of the patients served in that environment are absolute necessities. . . . [D]ifferent organizations and different patient populations will require greater or lesser tolerance for risk; an environment for one patient population will not be appropriate for another. Each organization should continually visit and revisit its tolerance for risk and changes in the dynamics of the patient population."[2]

Additional NAPHS environmental recommendations include the following:[3]

- Hinges and door closers should be designed so that nothing can be tied to them.

- Power cords should be removed where possible and shortened to minimum lengths to reduce opportunities for hanging.

- Glass should be tempered or polycarbonate, and mirrors should be polished metal.

- Grab bars in bathrooms should be removable and installed only when needed for a patient with medical necessity.

- Arm pulls should be mounted upside down.

- Push-pull latches are recommended rather than door knobs. These latches can be mounted upside-down to minimize risk.

- Door locks should be removed or designed to prevent a patient from locking himself or herself in a room.

If possible, doors should also open into corridors to prevent patients from barricading themselves in their rooms, and all light fixtures should be tamper-resistant. Fluorescent lights should not be accessible to patients, and incandescent bulbs should be shatter-resistant if they are accessible to patients.

Ceiling-mounted fire sprinklers should be installed so that they break away under a 50-pound load dropped from one inch, to prevent the possibility of hanging.

Clothing poles should be removed or designed to prevent something being tied around them. Consider a "J"-shaped design. Clothing hooks, if used, should have a break-away design. Likewise, break-away towel hooks should be used in lieu of towel bars. Use curtain rods and shower curtain rods (if curtains are used) that have a break-away design.

Medical gas outlets, if present, should be covered and tamper-proof.

## Case Study: Assess facilities for suicide risk

Since January 1995, The Joint Commission has reviewed 501 patient suicides, which just barely beat out wrong-site surgeries as the commission's top sentinel event. So perhaps it was inevitable that The Joint Commission, as part of its 2007 National Patient Safety Goals, introduced a new goal to reduce the risks of patient suicide.

The goal requires hospitals to identify patients at risk for suicide by using the following provisions:

- Conduct a risk assessment examining specific factors that may increase or decrease suicide risks

- Address suicidal patients' immediate safety needs and the most appropriate setting for their treatment

- Provide resources (e.g., a hotline) for individuals and their family members who are in crisis

Although it is up to medical staff to assess patients for suicide risk, the goal's requirements also reach into clinical and building-safety aspects of patient safety. Hospital safety committees may need to evaluate the physical features of a building or room to ensure that patients can't use items to harm themselves.

Committee members should ask two basic questions relevant to the goal:

**1. To which areas of our facility do the goal's provisions apply?**
**2. Within those areas, what are the risks?**

To determine where this goal applies, safety officers should obtain "data from surveillance rounds in which they identify which patients are suicide risks and where they are housed, evaluate those areas, implement risk-reduction strategies, and report their findings to the safety committee," says Elizabeth Di Giacomo-Geffers, RN, MPH, healthcare consultant at Di Giacomo-Geffers and Associates, in Trabuco Canyon, CA.

To better pinpoint suicide risks within those areas, Di Giacomo-Geffers suggests a methodical approach:

1. Identify the structural components of the facility (e.g., floors, corridors, and rooms).
2. Then divide the rooms into patient rooms and other areas.
3. Further divide patient rooms into bathrooms, mini-kitchens (if present), etc.

Safety officers must also work to secure all areas in which staff might hold a potentially suicidal patient. Although most suicidal patients remain confined to their own rooms, those diagnosed with a low suicide risk might be allowed to walk freely through some of the corridors.

Meanwhile, suicidal patients whom the hospital has recently admitted would usually be in rooms near nursing stations for closer monitoring.

"All those areas should be made safe," Di Giacomo-Geffers says.

Using a checklist is a convenient way for staff to regularly assess building-related suicide risks (see **Figure 8.3**).

| Figure 8.3 | SAMPLE CHECKLIST OF POTENTIAL PATIENT SUICIDE RISKS |
|---|---|

Use this sample checklist to determine whether your hospital's physical features and building systems minimize patient suicide risks
Selected areas and items to consider satisfactory/unsatisfactory:

❑ Windows should not have breakable panes

❑ Window handles should be recessed or flush-mounted

❑ Cover visible ceiling pipes with protective material

❑ Cover electrical outlets and install ground-fault circuit interrupters to stop the flow of electricity if patients tamper with the outlets

❑ Cover fire-alarm pull stations to prevent tampering

❑ Fire-safety equipment (e.g., strobe lights, exit signs, emergency backup lighting, and horns) shouldn't be installed so high that they are beyond the reach of staff, who would then be unable to release a patient hanging from such an item

❑ Place portable fire extinguishers in metal or recessed cabinets that staff can only open with a key

❑ Smoke alarms should be recessed into the wall or ceiling so patients can't damage them and set off an alarm

❑ Lights should be recessed into the wall or ceiling and covered or bolted in place

| Figure 8.3 |
|---|

## SAMPLE CHECKLIST OF POTENTIAL
## PATIENT SUICIDE RISKS (CONT.)

❑ Furniture should either be bolted to the floor or be heavy enough to prevent someone from throwing it

❑ Doors, especially in psychiatric units, should feature tamper-proof screws

❑ Doors should have a 6-inch-to-8-inch cut from their tops to prevent patients from hanging themselves by wedging a towel between the top of the door and the frame

❑ The HVAC system should feature tamper-proof screws

❑ Mirrors should be shatterproof

❑ Showerheads should be cone-shaped so that if a patient tries to loop an item over the showerhead, the item will slip off

❑ Attach shower curtain rods to walls to prevent a patient from easily taking a rod down and using it as a weapon

❑ Shower bars should break off under pressure

❑ Keep telephone cords and oxygen tubing to a minimum in risk areas

❑ Watch for clothing that can be linked together to form a noose (e.g., scarves and handkerchiefs)

❑ Clothes hangers should be connected to hooks secured with tamper-proof screws

| Figure 8.3 | SAMPLE CHECKLIST OF POTENTIAL PATIENT SUICIDE RISKS (CONT.) |

❏ Replace plastic garbage bags with paper bags to avoid suffocation risks

❏ Keep sheets and pillow cases under lock and key—suicidal patients could braid them and use them as nooses

❏ Avoid plastic shower curtains because of suffocation risks

❏ Sinks should be boxed in and not feature P-traps, which patients can use to hang themselves

❏ Keep housekeeping carts with chemicals in secure spots

❏ Bulletin boards should use Velcro to attach items, not thumbtacks

❏ Use paper cups and plates instead of glass or ceramic dishware

❏ Always count plastic utensils going in and out of a patient's room

❏ In therapy activity rooms, use nontoxic paints and account for sharp objects (e.g., scissors)

❏ Lock the kitchens of psychiatric units

❏ Toilets should either feature bolted lids or be recessed into walls to prevent hanging

❏ Avoid installing dropped ceiling panels, which patients can remove to access pipes above

| Figure 8.3 | **SAMPLE CHECKLIST OF POTENTIAL PATIENT SUICIDE RISKS (CONT.)** |

❏ Use plastic bath and shower hooks because they break away under a small amount of weight

❏ Ensure that patients can't obtain aerosol cans, which can be used to get high or as crude flamethrowers

❏ Restrict access to air fresheners, which contain toxic chemicals

Adapted from *Briefings on Hospital Safety*, December 2006.

The safety committee should review the checklist's findings on a monthly or quarterly basis, she says.

Safety officers shouldn't be afraid to develop their own solutions to deflect suicide risk.

Patrick Keller, director of plant operations for The Pines Residential Treatment Centers in Portsmouth, VA, takes a forward-thinking approach in conjunction with clinicians. Keller and his team start by asking the following five questions:

1. Can a patient break something in the room (e.g., a bed, set of curtains, bathroom hook, etc.)?

2. Are there any toxic substances in the facility that a patient could obtain and swallow?

3. Are there any structural vulnerabilities that will be difficult to repair quickly?

4. Will hardware or furniture fail to withstand prolonged use and abuse (e.g., a patient kicks a door until the lock breaks)?

5. Can an object increase the opportunity for a potential sentinel event?

A "yes" answer to any of the above questions would prompt close scrutiny of the situation at The Pines. Once Keller's staff members formulate a facilitywide security plan, they brainstorm and sometimes invent solutions, including the following:

**An anti-suicide door that eliminates hanging**—The door is made from expanded PVC, a lightweight, shatter- and crack-proof substance that one can cut or shape to necessary specifications. The door has large openings at the top and bottom so nothing can be wedged into the door frame, and a continuous hinge prevents patients from hanging anything between the door and the frame.

Also, a rubber gasket on the latch side of the door allows for patient privacy but prevents anything from being wedged between the door and the frame.

"It's a very simple design," Keller says. Joint Commission surveyors were satisfied with it, he says.

**Durable coverings for safety equipment**—Patients may try to set off the fire alarm to open doors to otherwise secure wards. The Pines covers safety equipment with Lexan boxes. Lexan is a plastic material, and when placed over a fire alarm pull station, the box dissuades patients from triggering the alarm.

**The 400-pound door**—This stocky door is made of reinforced steel with a magnetic strip running the length of the door. Patients can't kick the door in or dislodge it from its hinges.

**Hockey pucks bolted to doors**—This arrangement prevents patients from slamming a door against a wall or frame so hard that the force breaks the doorstop or doorknob.

**Special covers for air conditioners**—The covers are made of plywood, sheet material, and a protective grill, and they stop patients from accessing the electrical components of the appliance.

**Protective boxes for water coolers**—The unbreakable boxes guard against anyone trying to damage the cooler or abuse its contents.

**Special wedges on the top of furniture pieces**—The wedges deny patients any gaps from which to hang a noose.

**Rubber-coated stairs**—The rubber helps to prevent slips and falls, and may also decrease hard edges on the steps.

**Special de-escalation rooms**—Keller's facility pipes in soft, classical music and hangs pictures of nature on the walls to give the rooms a calming atmosphere.

Keller says his team meets with clinicians once a month to discuss safety issues. "They want to make sure the rooms are pleasant and that patients can't harm themselves," he says. "Usually, we achieve both goals."

Adapted from *Briefings on Hospital Safety*, December 2006

## Summary

The challenges of keeping patients' environments free from potential hazards are constant and evolving. Environmental safety is an ongoing process and should be monitored on a regular basis. It's important to remember that you can assess your environment and make improvements, but no facility will ever be completely suicide-proof.

Again, don't try to assess your physical plant and system risks and make all improvements alone: See how other facilities are doing it. Developing a network among regional organizations, Internet talk groups, and/or national associations to share ideas, challenges, and successes can help us all learn from each other and continue to foster innovation in keeping patients safe. (For additional suggestions, see Appendix A: Resources at the end of this book, and the case study on the following pages.)

# Endnotes

1. David M. Sine, CSP, ARM; and James M. Hunt, AIA, *Guidelines for the Built Environment of Behavioral Health Facilities*, PDF distributed by the National Association of Psychiatric Health Systems, *www.naphs.org.*

2. Ibid.

3. The complete NAPHS guidelines can be found at *www.naphs.org/Teleconference/documents/REV9editedFINAL_001.pdf*

4. David M. Sine, CSP, ARM; and James M. Hunt, AIA, *Guidelines for the Built Environment of Behavioral Health Facilities*, PDF distributed by the National Association of Psychiatric Health Systems, *www.naphs.org.*

# PREPARING FOR THE SUICIDE-PREVENTION TRACER

# PREPARING FOR THE SUICIDE-PREVENTION TRACER

Effective January 1, 2007, The Joint Commission began implementing program-specific tracers for its hospital, ambulatory, home care, behavioral healthcare, critical-access hospital, and long-term-care accreditation programs. For hospitals, lab integration and suicide prevention were the first two such tracers.

These program-specific tracers are in addition to the regular, individual patient tracers that surveyors already conduct, plus system tracers (e.g., data, medication), and the emergency management tracer added in 2006.

According to The Joint Commission, the new program-specific suicide-prevention tracer is designed to:

- Evaluate the effectiveness of the organization's suicide-prevention strategy

- Identify hospital process, and possible system-level issues, that contribute to suicide attempts

According to the commission, the goal of these tracers is to discover safety concerns within different levels and types of care. The tracers focus on important issues relevant to information (e.g., your priority focus areas and Center for Medicare and Medicaid Services requirements), and will "evaluate program-specific issues and compliance with relevant patient-safety standards.

The topics for the program-specific tracers were identified through a review of literature, research, input from the field, and subject matter experts, according to The Joint Commission.

## What a surveyor might look for

For the suicide tracer, a surveyor might give a scenario to the intensive care unit (ICU) staff, step-down unit staff, and possibly the psych nurse, such as the following:

A patient presents with an overdose:
- When the patient is transferred, what precautions do you take?
- Where do you transfer the patient?
- How do you manage the psych problems?

A woman presents with severe postpartum depression:
- How do staff members protect her?
- What does obstetrics do?
- What resources does the unit have?

The surveyor would examine an ICU room that was prepared for the patient. Then the surveyor would walk through the transfer process.

The Joint Commission has indicated that it plans to develop additional program-specific tracers in the future. Contact your Joint Commission representative or go to the commission's Web site, *www.jointcommission.org*, for more information.

Adapted from *Briefings on JCAHO*, December 2006.

## Mock tracer activities

Mock tracer activities done prior to survey can serve important functions beyond simply preparing for the new tracer—they can also allow hospitals to see how well they're already complying with the suicide risk assessment goal, gauge their preparedness for a potential suicide scenario, and educate staff about suicide risk assessment.

Missi Halvorsen, RN, BSN, senior consultant for accreditation at Baptist Health, a five-hospital healthcare system in northeast Florida, says one of the hospitals in the Baptist Health system recently completed a mock tracer for the new suicide-prevention survey. She offers these tips to facilities considering a program-specific mock tracer:

1. Determine where a potentially suicidal patient would be likely to enter your care. In many hospitals, this would be the ED. Therefore, your designated mock surveyor might ask an ER nurse or other emergency staff, "What would you do if a teenage patient is admitted to your ED who has attempted to slit his wrists, indicates he'll do it again, and is combative?"

Discussion points might include the following:

Beyond treating his physical wounds, what is our facility's policy for assessing and protecting suicidal patients? Discuss what kind of assessment would be needed:

- What indicators would cause ED personnel to escalate safety measures?

- What additional measures would be used in this scenario, such as holding the patient in a "safe room" or activating one-to-one monitoring?

- When reassessment should occur, and by whom

- What crisis hotlines or other resources are available to suicidal patients and their families

2. Add tracer "spin-offs" to staff competency related to suicide risk assessments and competencies to related activities such as

- restraint application and policies
- orders and assessment
- diversional activities
- competencies of security staff or "sitters" assigned to watch potentially suicidal patients

Another tracer spin-off could include laboratory-related issues such as drug screening, critical values, etc., says Halversen.

| Figure 9.1 | **TO PREPARE FOR THE PROGRAM-SPECIFIC SURVEY** |

❑ Conduct a mock survey. Use your findings to fine-tune your hospital's assessment policies and hone staff awareness of patient suicide risk.

❑ Have patient records readily available. The surveyor will want to review the record to ascertain what services your facility provides.

❑ Ensure that your facility has an assessment tool for screening patients for suicide risk. This should be nothing new for emergency departments—however, many hospitals have developed informal processes, and now they must be formalized.

❑ Make sure that all staff are familiar with the screening tool, and know when it should be applied, and by whom.

❑ Have data readily available that show how you've minimized environmental risks to ensure patient safety.

❑ Provide evidence that patients and their caregivers are given crisis-hotline information.

C H A P T E R    T E N

# FREQUENTLY ASKED QUESTIONS

# FREQUENTLY ASKED QUESTIONS

**Q: Does the suicide risk assessment NPSG apply to general hospitals?**

**A:** The Joint Commission has indicated that this goal applies to hospitals that provide psychiatric services and treat patients who present with a psychiatric condition. However, this goal has been subject to different interpretations. Contact your Joint Commission representative if you're uncertain, and request a written response to help avoid confusion at survey time.

**Q: Does the goal require us to screen patients in the acute-care setting if they have a terminal diagnosis?**

**A:** No. However, if patients with a terminal diagnosis are exhibiting suicidal ideation and/or behaviors, suicide risk would necessarily become a target for treatment and require many of the actions indicated by this NPSG.

**Q: We are a small rural hospital that doesn't have a behavioral facility on site, although we do see psychiatric patients in our Emergency Department. Does this NPSG apply to us?**

**A:** Yes. This goal would apply for your patients whose presenting problem is psychiatric or where the presenting injury or illness is known or presumed to be the result of a suicide attempt.

**Q: We're trying to develop a tool for assessing patient suicide risk. Where can we find resources to help us build one?**

**A:** Seek help from other facilities in your area, and see if their tools can be adapted for use in your organization. Several Web sites also offer information that can be helpful in developing a screening tool. Try the Suicide Prevention Resource Center, *www.sprc.org*; American Association of Suicidology, *www.suicidology.org*; American Foundation for Suicide Prevention, *www.afsp.org*; National Institute of Mental Health, Suicide Research Consortium, *www.nimh.gov/suicideresearch/consortium.cfm*; American Psychiatric Association, *www.psych.org*; or National Center for Injury Prevention, *www.cdc.gov/ncipc*. Your local Department of Mental Health may also offer resources and/or training programs.

A selection of resources for healthcare providers, patients, and family members is included in Appendix A at the back of this book.

**Q: Who should conduct the suicide risk assessment? Is that some-thing only a doctor can do, or can nurses also assess patients? Can admissions staff?**

**A:** Although a trained mental-health professional (psychiatrist, social worker, psychologist, psychiatric nurse, etc.) is the best choice to perform an in-depth suicide risk assessment, other staff members, including admission staff, can be trained to gather information in the form of an initial suicide risk screen (see Chapter 4). The screen could then trigger a further assessment as indicated, and this in-depth assessment would be conducted by the doctor, psychiatrist, a qualified nurse, social worker, or therapist. Your policies should include this information, and staff should understand who can conduct an initial screen and who can perform a more detailed follow-up assessment when required.

**Q: What should our policy be for patients in the ED who have attempted suicide, but are ambulatory?**

**A:** Most emergency departments have the potentially suicidal patient monitored on a one-to-one basis, whether by nursing staff, ER tech, or security staff. Others have patients assigned to rooms that are in direct line of sight of the nursing station. Still others designate a specifically designed "safe room" where psychiatric patients can be kept safe until their situation de-escalates or until they can be transferred to a psychiatric facility.

This question and related ones come up frequently on patient-safety-oriented list servers on the Web. Visit one of these forums and request information from other emergency departments.

**Q: How do you maintain one-to-one contact when the ED nurse has to handle three or four other patients?**

**A:** We have a safe room that's designed to accommodate suicidal patients. Security staff maintains visual surveillance on the patients in the safe room—this is the procedure in many hospitals.

If security is too busy and cannot do this, then the administrative supervisor is notified and a nursing assistant is assigned to ED to keep visual contact with the patient. (See Chapter 6 for more about one-to-one monitoring/staff mix.)

**Q: We are developing a suicide-risk assessment screen for our inpatients. What should our screen include?**

**A:** It depends on

- your patient population
- your treatment setting
- the qualifications of the staff who will be completing the screen.

The screen should identify high-risk factors, such as mental illness and substance abuse. The screen should also address the intent and lethality of the suicide plan.

Screens should be fine-tuned for certain patient populations. For example, some questions that have been shown effective to elicit suicide risk in a pediatric emergency department include

- "Have you been having thoughts about killing yourself in the past week?"
- "Are you here because you tried to hurt yourself?"
- "Have you ever tried to hurt yourself in the past other than this time?"
- "Has something very stressful happened to you in the past few weeks?"[1]

A screen aimed at adult populations would likely include questions about additional stressors—for example:

- "Have you recently lost a loved one?"
- "Have you lost your job in the past six months?"

**Q: We are not a behavioral heath organization, but deal with many overdoses and suicide attempts through our ED, and we do not have a psychiatrist on staff. We treat the physical wounds until patients are deemed stable enough to transfer to a psychiatric facility. When should we assess/reassess these patients?**

**A:** The suicidal patient should be assessed, at a minimum,

- at admission
- whenever there is a change in functioning/behavior
- prior to transfer

Regardless of when you decide to reassess, if it's specified in your policies, you must be able to show that you're following your policy consistently.

**Q: Should our Emergency Department suicide prevention policy be different from our hospitalwide policy?**

**A:** The suicide risk assessment goal carries the same requirements for any setting in which patients are being treated for psychiatric disorders. Depending on how these patients are treated in each area, the policies may differ somewhat. For example, an assessment policy for the ED might be to trigger an assessment at admission when injuries appear to be self-inflicted or the patient's presenting problem is psychiatric. An assessment for an admission might be to trigger an assessment at any time when a medical patient expresses suicidal ideation or attempts self-harm.

In the emergency department, the disposition may be to transfer to a psychiatric unit or hospital. For patients on medical units, transfer may not be possible until the medical condition is stabilized, so the suicidal risk must be managed on the unit.

**Q: We've heard of instances where patients have committed suicide in a facility, but were not identified as at-risk upon admission. If an initial review of systems indicates no triggers signaling thoughts of suicide, should we continue to reevaluate patients during their hospital stay?**

**A:** This question brings up a very important point: Many patients who complete suicide were not admitted for suicidal ideation or behaviors. When to reevaluate depends on your setting. For a non-psychiatric setting and patients who present with no significant psychiatric problems or risk factors, the patient would only need to be reassessed if his or her condition indicated it, such as a medical patient expressing suicidal thoughts some time after the initial assessment.

For psychiatric patients, suicide risk should be monitored routinely during hospitalization, when there has been any change in functioning, and again prior to discharge. Most, if not all, behavioral facilities are already doing so.

**Q: We're just starting our environment of care (EOC) assessment for suicide risk. Any suggestions for how we should proceed, or what to look for?**

**A:** First, you should recruit an interdisciplinary team, ideally one that includes front-line staff. Once you have your team, they should review data from Joint Commission sentinel events, your hospital incident reports, and other agencies such as state and county health agencies and similar organizations. After reviewing as much relevant information as possible, your team should be in a good position to assess your facility's environment of care.

The National Association of Psychiatric Health Systems has an excellent report with specific recommendations for EOC.[2]

**Q: Our small hospital doesn't have a psychiatric unit. We hold overdose cases, etc., on the med/surg floor until appropriate transfer or until cleared by the physician the next day. Can we use a behavioral health assessment or questions that could be used by med/surg. staff to help us evaluate these cases?**

**A:** Yes, but your screening or assessment tools will need to be appropriate for the level of training and scope of practice for the staff involved. Most med/surg staff should be able to gather basic information regarding suicide risk. The interpretation of these basic data can then be done by a trained nurse, social worker, or physician.

**Q: Our facilities risk assessment showed that we need to replace our current shower handles/knobs with suicide-proof bathroom fixtures (to prevent hanging). Where can we find suicide-proof fixtures?**

**A:** No fixtures are "suicide-proof," but many are designed specifically to reduce suicide risk. You can start by asking facilities managers at other sites for their recommendations, or by doing Web-based research. A good set of specific recommendations is available in *Guidelines for the Built Environment of Behavioral Health Facilities*, a white paper by David M. Sine, CSP, ARM, and James M. Hunt, AIA, at *www.naphs.org/ Teleconference/safetystandards.html#WhitePaper*. This comprehensive document includes suggestions, illustrations, manufacturers, and even recommended part numbers.

**Q: What should we include on a failure modes and effects analysis (FMEA) on inpatient suicide?**

**A:** An FMEA of inpatient suicide should include

- a review of available data from The Joint Commission sentinel events

- American Psychiatric Association treatment guidelines for assessing and managing suicidal behavior

- a review of pertinent literature

From there, any hospital incident report data should be reviewed, along with any incidents from other similar facilities. This review should elicit a list of probable root causes that can then be developed with respect to your particular setting.

At a minimum, include

- your current policies and procedures regarding suicide risk assessment and reassessment,

- policies regarding criteria for determining the appropriate level of care,

- interventions that address the immediate safety needs of the patient,

- EOC risk assessment,

- orientation and training materials,

- patient and family education, and

- discharge procedures.

See Chapter 7 for more about conducting an FMEA on patient suicide.

**Q: What does the Joint Commission look for in a suicide program-specific tracer?**

**A:** According to Joint Commission literature,[3] a surveyor will evaluate your hospital's suicide prevention strategy's effectiveness, and identify processes or system issues that may contribute to suicide attempts. Facility personnel involved in this tracer will include staff members and management who have been involved in the individual's care, treatment, or services

To prepare for this tracer, ensure that your facility has an assessment tool for screening patients for suicide risk; that your staff knows when to screen patients; and that staff members know what to do if an elevated suicide risk is indicated. Such an assessment tool should be nothing new for emergency departments; however, informal processes that are often used must now be formalized.

See Chapter 10 of this book, visit The Joint Commission's Web site (*www.jointcommission.org*) or read the November 2006 *Joint Commission Perspectives* newsletter for more about program-specific tracers.

**Q: Our ED see patients with suicidal ideation in addition to regular medical patients, and I'm trying to determine standard of care for the ED. Once a physician has determined the patient has suicidal ideation and places a sitter with the patient, is the patient allowed to use the restroom without direct observation? Does the door need to be slightly ajar, or is the patient required to use a bedpan?**

**A:** An actively suicidal patient should be monitored at all times. Having a sitter in the room while the patient uses the restroom with the door ajar should be sufficient. For someone who has actively continued to attempt self-harm while in the ED, "touching distance" monitoring may be indicated.

# Endnotes

1. Horowitz, L. M., P.S. Wang, G.P. Koocher, et al, "Detecting Suicide Risk in a Pediatric Emergency Department: Development of a brief screening tool," *Pediatrics* 107 no. 5 (2001).

2. Go to the National Association of Psychiatric Healthcare Systems Web site, at *www.naphs.org*, for more information; or the "Performance Measurement Initiatives" section of The Joint Commission's Web site, *www.jointcommission.org*.

3. From The Joint Commission's "Surveyor's Activity Guide," January 2007, available to Joint-Commission-accredited organizations, December 2006.

# APPENDIX A

## RESOURCES

# RESOURCES

Following are some of the available resources that can provide additional information regarding suicide prevention, sample assessment policies, and additional forms. This listing is intended as a sample, and is not comprehensive.

**American Association of Suicidology** (AAS)—This organization promotes research, public-awareness programs, public education, and training for professionals and volunteers. In addition, AAS serves as a national clearinghouse for information on suicide, and provides guidelines for suicide risk assessment, treatment and care. *www.suicidology.org*.

**American College of Emergency Physicians** (ACEP)—a national medical society with more than 23,000 members. ACEP is committed to advancing emergency care through continuing education, research, and public education. ACEP, based in Dallas, has 53 chapters representing each state, Puerto Rico, and the District of Columbia. *www.acep.org*.

**The Joint Commission**—The complete NPSG list, requirements, and additional compliance information can be found at The Joint Commission's Web site, *www.jointcommission.org*. Refer to the standards and scoring guidelines in The

Joint Commission's *Comprehensive Accreditation Manual for Hospitals* for descriptions of Joint Commission requirements and examples of compliance.

**National Alliance on Mental Illness** (NAMI)—This organization offers information, support, and advocacy for persons affected by mental illnesses. *www.nami.org*

**National Association of Psychiatric Health Systems** (NAPHS)—This association, founded in 1933, advocates for behavioral health and a commitment to responsive, accountable, and clinically effective prevention, treatment, and care for children, adolescents, adults, and older adults with mental and substance-abuse disorders. Members are behavioral healthcare provider organizations. *www.naphs.org.*

**National Institute of Mental Health** (NIMH)—This federal agency is a leader in research on mental and behavioral disorders. *www.nimh.nih.gov.*

**National Suicide Prevention Lifeline** (NSPL)—Provides resources for patients, families and healthcare providers, including "After an Attempt" brochures for each of these groups. The NSPL's informational Web site is located at *www.suicidepreventionlifeline.org.*

**Screening for Mental Health Inc.**—This private company provides "A resource guide for implementing the Joint Commission on Accreditation of Healthcare Organizations 2007 Patient Safety Goals on Suicide, featuring the Basic Suicide Assessment Five-Step Evaluation (B-SAFE)," a guide prepared by Douglas Jacobs, MD, CEO and president. *www.MentalHealthScreening.org.*

**Suicide and Mental Health International**—Founded by survivors left behind after suicide, this site offers a comprehensive global perspective on suicide assessment and prevention. It promotes the collection of complete, up-to-date, international data on issues of suicide and suicidal behavior. Members include suicide survivors, mental-health professionals and associates, physicians, nurses, etc. *www.smhai.org.*

**Suicide Prevention Action Network** (SPAN) USA—A national organization dedicated to action and advocacy for suicide prevention. 202/449-3600. *www.spanusa.org.*

**Suicide Prevention and Aftercare** (LINK–NRC)—Provides suicide-related community education in prevention, intervention, aftercare, and support. *www.thelink.org.*

**Suicide Prevention Resource Center**—Supports suicide prevention with the best of science, skills, and practice. 877/438-7772. *www.sprc.org.*

**U.S. Department of Health and Human Services**—The agency's Suicide Prevention and Resource Center offers information related to suicide assessment and prevention, news from states and other countries, as well as grant and funding information. *www.sprc.org/.*

## National hotlines

The third EP for the suicide risk assessment NPSG requires facilities to provide information about suicide prevention and available crisis hotlines to patients and families. Hospitals or systems that don't have their own 24-hour crisis hotline can provide a number to call for services in their area, or a national toll-free number. The following organizations provide access to trained telephone counselors, 24 hours a day, 7 days a week.

**National Hopeline Network**—800/784-2433, available around the clock, seven days a week. Callers are connected to crisis centers closest to their location. The Hopeline is sponsored by the Kristin Brooks Hope Center, based in Washington, D.C. Web site lists crisis centers for each state and additional resources. *www.hopeline.com.*

**The National Suicide Prevention Lifeline**—800/273-8255. This hotline, sponsored by the U.S. Department of Health and Human Services' Substance Abuse and Mental Health Services Administration (SAMHSA), is part of the National

Suicide Prevention Initiative, a collaborative effort led by SAMHSA that incorporates best practices and research findings in suicide prevention and intervention, with the goal of reducing the incidence of suicide nationwide.

**SuicideHotlines.net**—This Web site maintains an updated listing of local hotlines for suicide prevention and emotional-crisis support for each state. *http://suicidehotlines.net/index.html.*

## Demographic information

Below is a partial listing of suicide-related resources targeting specific population segments:

**American Academy of Pediatrics**—provides resources for pediatric suicide–risk assessment, including Lisa M. Horowitz, PhD, MPH, et al., "Detecting Suicide Risk in a Pediatric Emergency Department: Development of a Brief Screening Tool," *Pediatrics* 107 no. 5 (May 2001):1133-1137. *www.aap.org.*

**American Psychological Association** (APA)—The APA's Depression and Suicide in Older Adults Resource Guide Web site includes studies, journal articles, and a range of resources for older patients and their families. 202/336-6050. *www.apa.org/pi/aging/depression.html.*

**National Institute on Aging**—Provides health information, latest research findings, and scientific resources about aging and related issues. *www.nia.nih.gov/.*

**National Organization for People of Color Against Suicide**—Addresses and raises awareness about suicide in minority communities. 866/899-5317. *www.nopcas.com.*

**The Trevor Helpline**—866/4U-TREVOR. A national 24-hour, toll-free suicide prevention hotline that focuses on gay and questioning youth. *www.thetrevorproject.org.*

# BEYOND THE NPSG: RELATED STANDARDS IN THE *CAMH*

# BEYOND THE NPSG:
# RELATED STANDARDS IN THE *CAMH*

The suicide assessment NPSG is not the only suicide-related measure that Joint Commission-accredited facilities must meet. As earlier chapters indicated, The Joint Commission's *Comprehensive Accreditation Manual for Hospitals (CAMH)* includes a variety of standards spanning many chapters. These standards are related to the root causes of suicide.

Following is a list of suicide-related *CAMH* standards that hospitals must currently meet:

- **Environment of care (EC):**
    **EC.1.10** (written plan for managing safety risks)
    **EC.2.10** (safe environment)

- **Ethics, rights, and responsibilities (RI):**
    **RI.3.10** (patients are given information about their responsibilities)

- **Human resources (HR):**

    **HR.1.10** (adequate number/mix of staff)

    **HR.1.20** (qualifications meet job responsibilities)

    **HR.2.30** (ongoing education and training for competency)

- **Leadership (LD):**

    **LD.3.60** (effective organization communication)

- **Provision of care (PC):**

    **PC.2.130** (patients' initial assessments are completed thoroughly and on time)

    **PC.2.150** (patients are reassessed when appropriate)

    **PC.2.20** (organization defines data and information gathered in assessments and reassessments)

    **PC.3.130** (needs of patients receiving treatment for emotional or behavioral disorders are assessed)

    **PC.6.10** (education and training specific to needs and care, treatment, and services)

    **PC.15.10** (process addresses needs after discharge or transfer)

**PC.15.20** (transfer or discharge of patient to another level of care based on assessed needs and organization capabilities)

**PC.15.30** (upon transfer/discharge, information is exchanged with service providers)

Adapted from *Briefings on JCAHO*, September 2006.